THE NEW DIGITAL GOLD: A SIMPLE GUIDE TO CRYPTOCURRENCY

A BEGINNER'S MANUAL FOR LEARNING THE BASICS, BUYING, SELLING, STORING SAFELY, AVOIDING MISTAKES, AND BUILDING SMART INVESTMENT HABITS

MAXWELL WESTBROOK

Copyright © [Maxwell Westbrook. 2025] - All rights reserved.

The content contained within this book may not be reproduced, duplicated, or transmitted without direct written permission from the author or the publisher.

Under no circumstances will any blame or legal responsibility be held against the publisher or author for any damages, reparation, or monetary loss due to the information contained within this book. Either directly or indirectly. You are responsible for your own choices, actions, and results.

Legal Notice:

This book is copyright-protected. This book is only for personal use. You cannot amend, distribute, sell, use, quote, or paraphrase any part of this book's content without the author's or publisher's consent.

Disclaimer Notice:

Please note the information contained within this document is for educational and entertainment purposes only. All effort has been executed to present accurate, up-to-date, and reliable, complete information. No warranties of any kind are declared or implied. Readers acknowledge that the author does not render legal, financial, medical, or professional advice. The content within this book has been derived from various sources. Please consult a licensed professional before attempting any techniques outlined in this book.

By reading this document, the reader agrees that under no circumstances is the author responsible for any losses, direct or indirect, which are incurred as a result of the use of the information contained within this document, including, but not limited to, — errors, omissions, or inaccuracies.

DISCLAIMER

This book and its supplementary materials, including the compounding PDF, are designed to provide information and insights into cryptocurrency. While every effort has been made to ensure the accuracy, completeness, and reliability of the information provided, the author and publisher do not guarantee the accuracy or completeness of the content and disclaim all warranties, express or implied. By engaging with this book and its supplementary materials, you agree to the following:

1. Not Financial Advice

The content of this book is intended for educational purposes only and should not be considered financial advice., legal, tax, or investment advice. Readers should seek independent advice from a qualified financial advisor or professional before making investment or financial decisions.

2. Investment Risks

Investing in cryptocurrency involves significant risks, including, but not limited to, market volatility, liquidity issues, regulatory changes, technological risks, and potential loss of your entire investment. This book's examples, strategies, and scenarios are hypothetical and do not guarantee future results or performance. Readers should only invest funds they can afford to lose.

3. No Liability

The author and publisher accept no liability for any loss, damage, or disruption resulting directly or indirectly from reliance on the information presented in this book. This includes but is not limited to economic losses, legal disputes, or losses arising from technical or security failures.

4. Regulatory Uncertainty

Cryptocurrency laws and regulations vary by jurisdiction and are subject to change. It is the reader's responsibility to understand and comply with the rules and regulations in their region. The author and publisher are not responsible for any legal consequences from cryptocurrency or participation in related activities.

5. No Endorsements

The mention of specific cryptocurrencies, exchanges, platforms, or services in this book does not constitute endorsement or recommendation by the author or publisher. Readers must perform due diligence and research before engaging with third-party services or investments.

6. Forward-Looking Statements

This book may include forward-looking statements, which are inherently speculative and subject to risks and uncertainties. Actual outcomes may differ significantly from the scenarios or projections presented.

7. Author's Interest

The author may hold positions in some cryptocurrencies or digital assets discussed in this book. However, this does not influence the impartiality or integrity of the information provided.

By reading this book and its related materials, you acknowledge that you have read, understood, and accepted this disclaimer.

READY TO TAKE YOUR CRYPTO KNOWLEDGE FURTHER?

As you navigate the exciting world of cryptocurrency, you may want more clarity, tools, and confidence to make informed decisions. That's why I've created an **exclusive set of free resources** for readers of *The New Digital Gold*.

Here's what's waiting for you:

- A **Crypto Glossary** to simplify even the most confusing terms.
- A **Beginner's Guide to Compounding** to help you grow your investments.
- A **Quiz** to test and solidify your knowledge from this book.
- A curated **Resource Library** filled with trusted tools, apps, and links to save you time and effort.

But that's not all. You'll also gain **early access and exclusive discounts** on my next book by opting in, which will dive even deeper into the crypto world.

I want to ensure you have everything you need to succeed in this rapidly evolving space, and these free resources are my way of helping you stay ahead of the curve.

Don't miss out—this exclusive offer is only available to readers of this book. Head over now and join our growing community of empowered crypto enthusiasts.

CONTENTS

Introduction	11
1. UNDERSTANDING THE BASICS OF CRYPTOCURRENCY	15
1.1 What is Cryptocurrency? A Simple Explanation	15
1.2 The Evolution of Digital Currency: From Bitcoin to Altcoins	18
1.3 Blockchain Demystified: The Technology Behind Cryptocurrencies	20
1.4 Key Terminology: A Beginner's Glossary	24
1.5 Understanding the Cryptocurrency Market and Its Dynamics	27
1.6 Debunking Myths: Cryptocurrency as a Passing Trend	30
2. NAVIGATING THE CRYPTOCURRENCY LANDSCAPE	33
2.1 Choosing a Secure Cryptocurrency Exchange	34
2.2 Setting Up Your First Cryptocurrency Wallet	37
2.3 Security Measures: Protecting Your Digital Assets	39
2.4 Regulatory Considerations: What Beginners Need to Know	42
2.5 Avoiding Scams: Identifying Red Flags	44
2.6 The Role of Fiat in the World of Cryptocurrency	46
3. BUYING AND SELLING CRYPTOCURRENCY	51
3.1 Creating a Smart Cryptocurrency Investment Budget	52
3.2 Step-by-Step Guide to Buying Your First Cryptocurrency	54

3.3 Transferring your cryptocurrency to your wallet	56
3.4 Selling Cryptocurrency: Timing and Strategies	57
3.5 Understanding Transaction Fees and Costs	61
3.6 Tax Implications: Navigating the Legal Aspects	64
3.7 How to Avoid Common Mistakes When Trading	66
4. SAFEGUARDING YOUR INVESTMENTS	69
4.1 The Power of Diversification in Cryptocurrency Investing	69
4.2 Risk Management: Protecting Your Investments	72
4.3 Keeping Emotions in Check: Trading with Discipline	74
4.4 The Importance of Continuous Learning and Adaptation	77
4.5 Tools and Resources for Staying Informed	79
4.6 Case Studies: Learning from the Mistakes of Others	81
5. DEVELOPING A SMART INVESTMENT STRATEGY	87
5.1 Setting SMART Goals for Cryptocurrency Investing	87
5.2 Understanding Market Trends and Indicators	89
5.3 Long-Term vs. Short-Term Investment Approaches	92
5.4 The Four-Year Cycle: Timing Your Investments	94
5.5 Alt Season: Unlocking Opportunities in the Cryptocurrency Cycle	97
5.6 Leveraging Technology: Apps and Tools for Investors	100
5.7 Learning from Successful Investors: Best Practices and Tips	102
5.8 Learning from Failure: Lessons from Crypto Missteps	104

6. EXPLORING THE POTENTIAL OF BLOCKCHAIN TECHNOLOGY — 107
6.1 Transforming Industries with Blockchain Technology — 108
6.2 Smart Contracts: Automating Agreements — 110
6.3 Decentralized Finance (DeFi): The Next Frontier — 113
6.4 NFTs: The Intersection of Art and Technology — 116
6.5 Blockchain in Different Industries: Real-World Examples — 118
6.6 Anticipating Future Trends: Where is Blockchain Headed? — 121

7. ADDRESSING COMMON CONCERNS AND MISUNDERSTANDINGS — 125
7.1 Essential Security Measures for Protecting Your Digital Assets — 126
7.2 Cryptocurrency and Environmental Impact: The Truth — 129
7.3 Overcoming the Fear of Missing Out (FOMO) — 131
7.4 The Role of Community: Finding Support and Resources — 133
7.5 Critically Evaluating Cryptocurrency News and Trends — 136
7.6 Understanding Black Swan Events in Cryptocurrency — 139

8. BUILDING CONFIDENCE FOR FUTURE INVESTMENTS — 141
8.1 The Importance of Lifelong Learning in Cryptocurrency — 141
8.2 Opportunities for Career Advancement in Cryptocurrency — 143
8.3 Balancing Cryptocurrency with Other Financial Priorities — 146
8.4 Developing Critical Thinking Skills for Better Decision-Making — 148
8.5 Inspiring Stories: Success and Lessons from Investors — 151

| Conclusion | 153 |
| References | 157 |

INTRODUCTION

Not long ago, a friend of mine, curious about the buzz surrounding cryptocurrency, decided to dive in. Armed with enthusiasm but little else, she invested in a popular digital coin. A few weeks later, she was overwhelmed by market fluctuations and technical jargon. She called me, frustrated and confused, unsure if she had made a mistake. This scenario is all too common for beginners, who often find themselves swept into the excitement without a clear understanding of the landscape.

This book aims to change that. Its purpose is to demystify cryptocurrency for those starting their journey. Here, you will find a simple guide to understanding, buying, selling, and safely storing digital currencies. We aim to turn confusion into clarity, empowering you to make informed decisions.

The vision for this book is to equip you with the knowledge and confidence needed to navigate the cryptocurrency world independently. A solid understanding is crucial for creating investment strategies that align with your goals. This book serves as a foundation, building your awareness to explore confidently.

At the heart of this book lies a simple thesis: cryptocurrency is accessible to everyone. You do not need a vast fortune or extensive knowledge to begin investing. The digital currency market offers opportunities for financial growth, regardless of your starting point.

Throughout the book, we will explore several key themes. We will trace the evolution of digital currency and discuss the importance of security and regulation. We will also examine how cryptocurrency can empower individuals financially, opening doors that traditional systems may not.

The book is structured to guide you step-by-step, with each chapter building on the last to gradually expand your understanding. We include practical examples and case studies to illustrate key points. As a free bonus, we've provided a glossary of essential terms and jargon to help you get familiar with the language of cryptocurrency right away.

Many new investors are concerned about entering this market. The volatility of cryptocurrency and the complexity of blockchain technology can seem daunting. This book addresses these fears, presenting information in a straightforward manner that is easy to grasp and apply.

It will help you make informed decisions and avoid common pitfalls. This book is a stepping stone toward financial literacy and independence.

I encourage you to engage with the content actively. Apply what you learn and approach cryptocurrency with an open mind and strategic outlook. View this journey as an opportunity for growth and empowerment. The digital currency landscape is vast and full of potential.

Allow me to introduce myself. I have a deep passion for helping beginners navigate the complexities of cryptocurrency. With years of experience and a commitment to financial literacy, I aim to provide reputable and easy-to-follow guidance.

Let us embark on this journey together. The cryptocurrency world holds promise and potential. With knowledge and understanding, you can succeed and thrive. Embrace the possibilities that lie ahead with excitement and optimism. Your adventure in the digital currency world begins here.

CHAPTER 1
UNDERSTANDING THE BASICS OF CRYPTOCURRENCY

A few years ago, I met a young entrepreneur named Alex, who had just started his own business. He was determined to accept cryptocurrency as a form of payment, believing it to be the future of transactions. However, Alex soon found himself puzzled by the intricate web of terms and technology. His initial excitement turned into hesitation as he realized how little he understood about the digital currency world. This is a common experience as many people are intrigued by the potential of cryptocurrency but are daunted by its complexity. This chapter will guide you through the basics, providing a clear and understandable foundation to confidently engage with this evolving financial realm.

1.1 WHAT IS CRYPTOCURRENCY? A SIMPLE EXPLANATION

Cryptocurrency, at its core, is a form of digital currency. Unlike cash or coins you might carry in your wallet, they exist only in digital form. Meaning no physical bills or coins are involved. Instead, it operates entirely online, utilizing complex algorithms to maintain security and integrity. Decentralization is a key feature of cryptocurrency, which means it is not controlled by any central authority, like a bank or government. Instead, it relies on a network of computers, known as nodes, to manage and record transactions. This decentralization offers transparency and security not seen in traditional currencies. Peer-to-peer transactions are another hallmark of cryptocurrency. These transactions enable individuals to transfer payments directly to each other without the need for intermediaries such as banks. This direct interaction can significantly reduce transaction fees and processing times.

Understanding these basic concepts is crucial for anyone looking to enter the world of cryptocurrency. Grasping these fundamentals will give you the confidence to make informed decisions as you begin to explore more advanced topics. By establishing a solid foundation, you ease your entry into investing and lay the groundwork for further learning. Cryptocurrency was created with a purpose in mind. One of its primary goals is to provide financial independence from traditional banking systems. Many worldwide lack access to these systems, and cryptocurrency offers a viable alternative. It also provides global accessibility, allowing anyone with an internet connection to participate. This inclusivity is a powerful feature that can help drive financial empowerment. Cryptocurrencies often come with reduced transaction fees compared to traditional banking, making them an attractive option for cost-conscious individuals.

Comparing cryptocurrency to traditional currencies is helpful for better understanding. Consider gold, which has long been seen as a store of value. Cryptocurrency, sometimes referred to as digital gold, shares this characteristic. However, it exists in a digital space, accessible anywhere at any time. This digital nature means storage is also different. Instead of a physical vault, you store your cryptocurrency in a digital wallet. These differences highlight how cryptocurrencies can offer new opportunities and conveniences that traditional currencies may not provide.

It's essential to address some common misconceptions about cryptocurrencies. Many people believe you need to be tech-savvy to understand or use them, which is untrue. While a basic understanding of technology can be helpful, it is not required to participate in the cryptocurrency market. Others view cryptocurrencies as merely speculative investments akin to gambling. While their value can be volatile, they offer more than just a chance for profit. They're tools for financial empowerment and innovation. Some associate cryptocurrencies with illegal activities due to their early use in such contexts. However, they have gained legitimacy and legality in many mainstream applications. Today, cryptocurrencies are becoming increasingly accepted by businesses and governments worldwide.

This chapter lays the groundwork for your understanding of cryptocurrency. By clarifying the fundamental concepts and addressing misconceptions, you are better equipped to explore and engage with this dynamic and exciting field. As you continue through this book, you will build on this knowledge, gaining the skills and confidence needed to navigate the cryptocurrency landscape effectively.

1.2 THE EVOLUTION OF DIGITAL CURRENCY: FROM BITCOIN TO ALTCOINS

The cryptocurrency story begins with the mysterious figure known as Satoshi Nakamoto, whose identity remains unknown. In 2008, Nakamoto released a whitepaper titled "Bitcoin: A Peer-to-Peer Electronic Cash System." This document laid out the foundation for what would become the first cryptocurrency: Bitcoin. The whitepaper envisioned a decentralized digital currency that enabled peer-to-peer transactions without needing trusted third parties like banks. In January 2009, the inaugural Bitcoin transaction was completed, marking the birth of this revolutionary currency. Nakamoto mined the "genesis block," which contained the first 50 bitcoins. This event set the stage for a financial innovation that would challenge traditional monetary systems. Bitcoin's introduction was more than just a technological advancement; it was a response to the global economic crisis of 2008, offering an alternative to the established financial order.

As Bitcoin gained popularity, it paved the way for the emergence of alternative cryptocurrencies, commonly referred to as altcoins. These new digital currencies were developed to address specific limitations or to introduce new functionalities that Bitcoin didn't offer. Ethereum, for example, introduced the idea of smart contracts—self-executing agreements where the terms are embedded directly into the code. Ethereum's innovation allowed more complex transactions to occur automatically on the blockchain, opening doors to decentralized applications. Litecoin, another significant altcoin, focused on transaction speed. It was created to validate transactions faster than Bitcoin, making it more suitable for daily use. Ripple, on the other hand, aimed to facilitate seamless transactions between banks. Its protocol enabled instant and secure cross-border payments, making it attractive to financial institutions.

When comparing altcoins to Bitcoin, several key differences and similarities emerge. Bitcoin and most altcoins use consensus mechanisms to validate transactions and secure the network. Bitcoin relies on a proof-of-work system, where miners solve intricate mathematical puzzles to add new blocks to the blockchain. Ethereum, however, is transitioning to a proof-of-stake model, where validators are chosen according to the number of coins they hold and are ready to "stake" as collateral. This change seeks to lower energy consumption and enhance scalability. In terms of use cases, Bitcoin is primarily seen as a store of value, much like digital gold. Many altcoins, like Ethereum, serve as platforms for innovative blockchain applications, while others, like Ripple, focus on specific industries like banking.

To understand the market dynamics of Bitcoin, one must consider the four-year cycle theory. This concept revolves around the Bitcoin "halving" events, occurring approximately every four years. The reward for mining new blocks is cut in half during a halving. This decrease in supply is intended to manage inflation and replicate the scarcity of precious metals such as gold. Historically, each halving has been followed by a significant increase in Bitcoin's price as investors anticipate a supply shortage. These cycles have become a focal point for traders and analysts, who use them to predict market trends and potential price movements. The four-year cycle theory highlights the interplay between supply, demand, and market psychology, offering a lens through which to view Bitcoin's price fluctuations.

The transition from Bitcoin to altcoins highlights the flexibility and innovation embedded in the cryptocurrency ecosystem. Each new development builds upon the last, addressing challenges and expanding possibilities. As we explore these digital currencies' histories, we see a landscape rich with potential and promise, continually adapting to satisfy the needs of its users. This constant evolution reflects a broader trend toward financial innovation that challenges traditional systems and empowers individuals with new tools for managing their wealth.

1.3 BLOCKCHAIN DEMYSTIFIED: THE TECHNOLOGY BEHIND CRYPTOCURRENCIES

To appreciate the transformative power of cryptocurrencies, one must first understand blockchain technology, the foundational architecture that supports these digital assets. Picture a blockchain as a digital ledger, similar to a traditional accounting book, but with some key differences. Instead of pages, the ledger comprises blocks, each containing a list of transactions. The blocks are connected in chronological order, creating a chain that is both secure and transparent. Think of each block as a box filled with transaction data, sealed with a unique digital signature known as a hash. This hash is a complex string of characters generated by a mathematical algorithm, ensuring that any alteration to the transaction data also changes the hash. Thus, the blockchain's design makes it nearly impossible to alter past transactions without detection, as each block's hash depends on the one before.

Verifying transactions on a blockchain involves intricate yet fascinating mechanisms known as mining and consensus. In the world of Bitcoin, mining refers to the method through which transactions are confirmed and added to the public ledger. Using powerful computers, Miners solve complex mathematical puzzles to validate a block of transactions. This process, known as proof of work, requires significant computational power and energy. Once a block is verified, it is incorporated into the chain, and the miner is rewarded with cryptocurrency. However, proof of work is not the only consensus mechanism available. Proof of stake provides an alternative method, where validators are chosen according to the volume of coins they hold, a process called staking. This method is seen as less energy-intensive and is being adopted by several blockchain networks. By staking, participants have a strong incentive to act ethically because they risk losing their staked coins if they do not.

Blockchain technology brings with it a host of benefits that surpass traditional systems. One of its most celebrated features is transparency. Every transaction is recorded and available for anyone to view, providing a level of openness that is impossible in conventional banking. This transparency is coupled with robust security. Thanks to its decentralized nature, altering a transaction on the blockchain would require an unlikely feat of changing it on every single node in the network simultaneously. Furthermore, blockchain ensures immutability, meaning once a transaction is recorded, it cannot be altered or removed. This permanence fosters trust, as users can be confident that the transaction history is accurate and tamper-proof.

Despite its advantages, blockchain is often misunderstood. A common misconception is that blockchain is used exclusively for financial transactions. In reality, its applications extend far beyond finance. It can be employed in various industries, from supply chain management to healthcare, where it ensures data integrity and authenticity. Another frequent misunderstanding is that blockchain transactions are always anonymous. While it is true that the identities behind transactions can remain hidden, the transactions themselves are visible to all. This pseudo-anonymity can offer privacy, but it also allows for scrutiny and verification by the network. Thus, blockchain is not the clandestine tool it is sometimes portrayed as, but rather a transparent and secure platform with vast potential.

Blockchain technology is fundamental to cryptocurrencies' performance, yet its reach extends beyond digital currency. By providing a transparent, secure, and immutable ledger, it has the potential to revolutionize various sectors. Understanding blockchain demystifies the complexities of cryptocurrencies and reveals the broader impact this innovation can have on society. As we continue to explore the cryptocurrency landscape, recognizing the foundational role of blockchain will deepen our appreciation for its current applications and future possibilities.

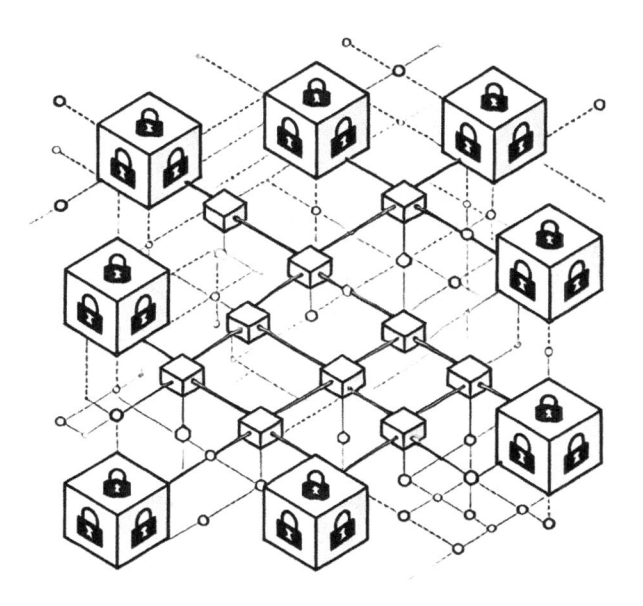

UNDERSTANDING THE BASICS OF CRYPTOCURRENCY 23

1.4 KEY TERMINOLOGY: A BEGINNER'S GLOSSARY

As you embark on your cryptocurrency exploration, you will encounter many terms that may initially seem daunting. However, understanding these key terms is beneficial and necessary for navigating the complex world of digital currencies. Let's begin with the term "wallet." In cryptocurrency, a wallet is a digital tool that stores your digital assets, much like an everyday wallet that holds your cash and credit cards. It doesn't physically store cryptocurrencies but keeps the private keys needed to access them on the blockchain. Wallets are available in different formats, such as software applications, online platforms, and hardware devices. Each type offers different degrees of security and convenience, giving you the flexibility to choose according to your needs and preferences.

Next, we recap "mining," a foundational concept in the cryptocurrency ecosystem. Mining is the procedure of verifying and recording transactions onto the public ledger, called the blockchain. In simple terms, miners use high-performance computers to solve difficult mathematical puzzles. This action not only validates transactions but also secures the network. In exchange, miners receive newly minted cryptocurrency as a reward, making mining a vital service and a lucrative endeavor for those with the necessary resources.

"ICO," or Initial Coin Offering, refers to a fundraising method used by new cryptocurrency projects. Equivalent to an Initial Public Offering (IPO) in the stock market, an ICO enables investors to participate in a new cryptocurrency venture, often with the anticipation of significant returns.

However, ICOs come with substantial risks, and potential investors should exercise due diligence.

Cryptography is the practice of securing communication and information by transforming them into an unreadable format to protect them from unauthorized access, using techniques like encryption, decryption, and digital signatures. It ensures the privacy, integrity, and authenticity of data.

The distinction between "cryptocurrency" and "token" often leads to confusion. Cryptocurrency refers to digital or virtual currencies that rely on cryptography for security, including Bitcoin and Ethereum. On the other hand, a token represents a unit of value issued on an existing blockchain. Tokens can serve various purposes, from granting access to a service to representing ownership in a project. Similarly, the terms "altcoin" and "stablecoin" can be perplexing. Altcoins are cryptocurrencies that are not Bitcoin. They provide a variety of features and use cases. On the other hand, stablecoins are designed to reduce price volatility by tying their value to a stable asset, such as the U.S. dollar. This makes them an appealing option for those who want the advantages of cryptocurrency without the dramatic price fluctuations.

A meme coin is a type of cryptocurrency typically created as a joke or based on internet memes and pop culture trends rather than having a serious technological or financial purpose. These coins quickly gain popularity due to social media hype and community support. Examples include Dogecoin and Shiba Inu. While meme coins can experience rapid price fluctuations, they are generally considered highly speculative and risky investments.

Cryptocurrency lingo is rich with slang that often leaves beginners scratching their heads. "HODL," a misspelled version of "hold," is a popular term that encourages investors to hold onto their assets regardless of market fluctuations. This term originated from a forum post during a Bitcoin price crash and has since become a rallying cry for long-term investors. "FOMO," or Fear of Missing Out, describes the anxiety one might feel when seeing others profiting from investments they have not made. It serves as a cautionary reminder to make informed decisions rather than act impulsively.

Prioritizing security is essential in the digital currency world, as well as understanding terms related to safety. "Two-factor authentication" (2FA) is a security measure that adds an extra layer of protection to your accounts. It requires not only a username and password but also something only the user possesses, such as a piece of information they should know or have immediately to hand, such as a physical token. "Cold storage" refers to the practice of storing your cryptocurrency offline to safeguard it from online threats. This method is considered one of the safest ways to store digital assets, as it prevents hackers from accessing your funds.

By familiarizing yourself with these terms, you equip yourself with the language of cryptocurrency, enhancing your ability to engage with the community and make informed decisions. This glossary serves as a stepping stone, enabling you to delve deeper into the exciting possibilities that digital currencies offer. Throughout the book, we elaborate further on many of these terms.

1.5 UNDERSTANDING THE CRYPTOCURRENCY MARKET AND ITS DYNAMICS

The cryptocurrency market is a dynamic and frequently unpredictable space where digital assets are exchanged. At the heart of this market are exchanges, which serve as platforms where buyers and sellers meet to trade cryptocurrencies. These exchanges operate like stock markets, allowing individuals to buy, sell, and sometimes even hold digital assets. They exist in different formats, such as centralized exchanges, which are operated by companies acting as intermediaries, and decentralized exchanges, which function and operate without a central authority, allowing users to trade directly with each other. Market makers are essential in this ecosystem as they supply liquidity. They accomplish this by placing buy and sell orders for a particular cryptocurrency, ensuring there is always a market for trading. This activity helps stabilize prices and narrow the spread between buying and selling prices, making transactions more efficient and accessible for all participants.

Volatility is a defining feature of the cryptocurrency market, often causing significant price swings that can occur in minutes. This volatility is primarily driven by speculation, as traders try to forecast future price movements by analyzing market trends and sentiment. Unlike traditional markets, where prices are influenced by predictable factors such as company earnings or economic indicators, the crypto market is more susceptible to shifts in investor sentiment and speculative trades. Regulatory news also contributes to volatility. When governments announce new regulations or policies regarding cryptocurrency, it can lead to sudden changes in investor confidence, causing prices to fluctuate rapidly. For instance, a government crackdown on crypto trading in one country can send shockwaves across the global market, affecting prices worldwide.

Retail money can significantly impact cryptocurrency volatility, and several key factors drive this effect. Retail investors often drive market sentiment, and their behavior is frequently speculative. When retail investors enter the market, they may do so based on hype, news, or social media trends rather than fundamental analysis. This leads to large price swings, especially without institutional investors who might provide stability. An example of positive market sentiment can be retail investors rushing into cryptocurrency after hearing about it on social media (e.g., the "Dogecoin pump" driven by retail enthusiasm). Conversely, negative news or rumors can cause retail investors to panic sell, exacerbating downturns and driving up volatility. Retail investors often follow each other, a phenomenon known as "herding." When a large group of retail investors makes similar moves, such as buying or selling a particular cryptocurrency, it can lead to rapid price movements. Their collective behavior, speculative trading patterns, herding instincts, and sometimes lack of market experience make the market more susceptible to wild price swings.

To navigate this volatile environment, traders rely on several market indicators to make informed decisions. Market capitalization, also known as market cap, is a vital metric that indicates the overall value of a cryptocurrency. The current price is multiplied by the total circulating supply of coins. A higher market cap often indicates a more established or trusted cryptocurrency. Trading volume is another crucial indicator, representing the total amount of a cryptocurrency traded over a specific period. High trading volume can signal strong interest or momentum in a particular coin, while low volume might suggest a lack of interest or liquidity. Traders use these indicators and others to assess a cryptocurrency's health and potential, helping them make strategic decisions in buying or selling.

External factors can profoundly impact the cryptocurrency market, often leading to unpredictable price movements. Government regulations, for example, can either bolster or undermine investor confidence. Positive regulatory developments can increase investment and price appreciation. An example of this could be legalizing cryptocurrency trading in a new region. Conversely, restrictive policies or outright bans can cause panic selling and sharp price declines. Technological advancements also have a major impact on shaping the market. Blockchain technology innovations or new features in a cryptocurrency can trigger increased interest and investment. On the other hand, technological setbacks, such as security breaches or network failures, can result in a loss of trust and a decrease in value.

The cryptocurrency market is a dynamic and intricate landscape influenced by a range of internal and external factors. Understanding how exchanges and market makers operate provides insight into the mechanics of trading, while awareness of market volatility and indicators helps make informed decisions. Recognizing the impact of external factors further adds depth to this understanding, highlighting the multifaceted nature of cryptocurrency investment. This comprehensive view of the market dynamics equips you with the tools to navigate digital currency's unpredictable yet rewarding world.

1.6 DEBUNKING MYTHS: CRYPTOCURRENCY AS A PASSING TREND

The idea that cryptocurrency is merely a passing trend often overlooks the significant evidence of its staying power in the global financial ecosystem. One of the strongest indications of its permanence is the substantial institutional investment pouring into the market. Major financial institutions like JPMorgan and Goldman Sachs have acknowledged cryptocurrencies' potential and begun offering their clients bitcoin-related services. This institutional backing provides legitimacy and stability that counters the notion of cryptocurrencies being a mere fad. Furthermore, the adoption by major companies, such as Tesla's investment in bitcoin and PayPal's integration of cryptocurrency transactions, underscores the growing acceptance of digital currencies in mainstream business operations. These moves signal a shift in the corporate world's approach to cryptocurrency, treating it as a viable asset class rather than a speculative gamble.

Cryptocurrencies are also becoming increasingly integrated into everyday financial interactions. Payment gateways now allow for the seamless use of digital currencies in transactions, making it easier for consumers to spend their crypto at various online and physical retailers. This integration into daily payments shows how cryptocurrencies are moving beyond speculative investments to become functional tools for commerce. Moreover, the rise of NFTs, or non-fungible tokens, represents a new frontier in digital ownership and art. Artists leverage NFTs to sell digital art directly to consumers, bypassing traditional galleries and auction houses. This democratizes the art market and illustrates how cryptocurrency technology can create new economic opportunities in creative industries. The expansion of use cases in everyday life highlights the versatility and adaptability of cryptocurrencies, reinforcing their relevance in modern financial systems.

Skepticism about cryptocurrencies, labelling them as a temporary craze, often draws parallels with past technological advancements that initially faced similar doubts. For instance, the internet was once dismissed as a fad, yet it has become integral to daily life and business. Like the early days of the internet, cryptocurrencies are experiencing growing pains and skepticism. However, their potential to revolutionize financial systems is undeniable. The historical trajectory of the internet serves as a reminder of how transformative technologies can evolve from niche interests to ubiquitous tools. This parallel underscores the potential for cryptocurrencies to follow a similar path of widespread adoption and integration into daily life.

The future potential and ongoing innovations within the cryptocurrency space further invalidate the notion of it being ephemeral. Decentralized Finance (DeFi) is one such development that promises to reshape traditional financial systems. DeFi platforms provide an array of financial services, such as lending, borrowing, and trading, all without the need for traditional intermediaries. This decentralization empowers users by giving them more control over their financial interactions, potentially reducing costs and increasing accessibility. Central Bank Digital Currencies (CBDCs) are gaining traction worldwide as governments explore digital versions of their national currencies. These state-backed digital currencies could coexist with current cryptocurrencies, further legitimizing and integrating digital currency into the global economy. The exploration of CBDCs by major economies like China and the European Union signals a willingness to adopt digital currency nationally, indicating a future where digital and traditional currencies work in tandem.

In summary, the evidence of institutional investments, the increasing integration of cryptocurrencies into everyday life, and the innovative developments within the crypto space collectively challenge the view of cryptocurrency as a fleeting trend. These factors highlight a continuous evolution that parallels past technological advancements, suggesting that cryptocurrencies are here to stay. As you continue to explore the vast potential of digital currencies, it becomes clear that they represent not just a momentary trend but a significant shift in the way we understand and interact with money. The possibilities are vast, and the future is bright for those willing to embrace this digital revolution.

CHAPTER 2
NAVIGATING THE CRYPTOCURRENCY LANDSCAPE

I magine Sarah, an eager investor ready to buy her first cryptocurrency. She's excited about the potential returns and the promise of decentralized finance, yet she finds herself stumped when choosing the right exchange. With countless options, each claiming to be the best, Sarah is overwhelmed. She wonders which platform offers security, ease of use, and value for money. This chapter is designed to guide you, like Sarah, through the essential steps of selecting a reputable cryptocurrency exchange, ensuring you make informed choices in this complex landscape.

2.1 CHOOSING A SECURE CRYPTOCURRENCY EXCHANGE

Choosing a secure exchange is a critical first step in your cryptocurrency journey. The importance of strong security protocols cannot be overstated. These protocols are the backbone of a trustworthy platform, protecting your assets from cyber threats. Look for exchanges that offer two-factor authentication, encryption, and cold storage of funds. These features reduce the risk of unauthorized access and potential loss of your assets. Moreover, a user-friendly interface is crucial, especially for beginners. An intuitive platform makes it easier to navigate the complexities of trading, allowing you to focus on strategy rather than struggling with complicated layouts. High liquidity is another key characteristic of a reputable exchange. It ensures you can buy and sell cryptocurrencies quickly without significant price fluctuations. Liquidity also indicates the presence of active traders, contributing to a vibrant and efficient market environment.

The choice between centralized and decentralized exchanges presents another consideration. Centralized exchanges, like Coinbase and Kraken, are operated by companies providing a trading platform. They offer user-friendly interfaces and often include additional services such as customer support and insurance for your funds. However, using a centralized exchange means entrusting your private keys to the platform, which could leave your assets vulnerable if the exchange were compromised. On the other hand, decentralized exchanges, such as Bisq, offer greater control over your private keys, as transactions occur directly between users without an intermediary. This model enhances privacy and reduces the risk of hacking but may also require a higher level of technical proficiency to navigate. Additionally, decentralized exchanges often lack the regulatory compliance found in centralized platforms, which can affect your transactions' legal and security aspects.

Evaluating fees and transaction costs is essential when choosing an exchange. Different platforms have varying fee structures, impacting your overall profit margins. Trading fees are charged when you buy or sell cryptocurrencies and can be a flat rate or a percentage of the transaction. Some exchanges also implement a maker-taker model, where you pay different fees based on whether you add liquidity to the market (maker) or take liquidity away (taker). Withdrawal fees are another consideration, as they can add up over time, especially if you frequently transfer funds to your wallet. By carefully assessing these costs, you can choose an exchange that offers the best value for your trading needs.

You should not underestimate the importance of customer support and reputation. A platform with responsive support can be invaluable when you encounter issues or have questions. Look for exchanges that offer multiple support channels, such as chat, email, or phone, and have a reputation for timely and helpful responses. Additionally, online reviews and community feedback can provide insights into the reliability and trustworthiness of an exchange. Engaging with user forums or social media discussions can help you gauge the experiences of other traders, allowing you to make an informed decision based on real-world feedback.

Exchange Evaluation Checklist

- Security Features: Does the exchange use two-factor authentication and encryption? Are funds stored in cold wallets?
- Usability: Is the platform intuitive and easy to navigate for beginners?
- Liquidity: Can you easily buy and sell cryptocurrencies without significant price changes?
- Fee Structure: What are the trading and withdrawal fees? Is there a maker-taker model?
- Customer Support: Are multiple support channels available? What do user reviews say about response times?
- Reputation: What feedback does the community provide about the exchange's reliability and trustworthiness?

Understanding these aspects will empower you to make choices that align with your goals and risk tolerance.

2.2 SETTING UP YOUR FIRST CRYPTOCURRENCY WALLET

Imagine you're about to step into the world of digital currency, and your first task is setting up a secure space to store your assets. This space is known as a cryptocurrency wallet, and understanding the types available can guide you in making the right choice. Hardware wallets are a popular option for those prioritizing security. These physical devices, like Ledger or Trezor, store your private keys offline, making them highly resistant to cyber-attacks. They're perfect for those who plan to hold their cryptocurrencies long-term. However, while protecting against online threats, they must be protected from physical damage.

In contrast, software wallets are programs or apps on your smartphone or computer. They offer convenience for those who need to access their funds regularly, making them suitable for active traders. These wallets connect to the internet, which makes them more vulnerable to hacks than hardware wallets. Therefore, they should be used cautiously and only for storing amounts you plan to trade frequently. Then, there are paper wallets, which involve printing your public and private keys on paper. They are entirely offline, thus immune to cyber threats. However, they pose a risk of physical loss or damage, requiring careful storage.

Setting up a cryptocurrency wallet involves a few straightforward steps. Begin by choosing a wallet type that suits your needs. If you opt for a software wallet, download the software from a reputable source, ensuring it's the official site to avoid malicious copies. Once installed, the wallet will generate a recovery phrase, often consisting of 12 or 24 random words. This phrase is crucial; it acts as a backup in case you lose access to your wallet. Write it down and store it securely, away from prying eyes. Losing this phrase means losing access to your funds. After securing your recovery phrase, your wallet is ready for use. Add cryptocurrencies by transferring them from an exchange, and you can start managing your digital assets.

Securing and backing up your wallet data is paramount. Regular updates are essential for maintaining security, as they protect against vulnerabilities that hackers might exploit. Ensure that your wallet software is always up to date. Two-factor authentication (2FA) adds another layer of security. It requires a second verification form beyond your password, such as a code sent to your mobile device. This step significantly reduces the risk of unauthorized access. Backing up your wallet, especially during the recovery phase, ensures that you can recover your funds if your device is lost or stolen. Consider storing backups in multiple secure locations to mitigate the risk of loss or damage.

Understanding the difference between hot and cold storage can help you manage your assets effectively. Hot storage refers to wallets connected to the internet, like software wallets. They provide easy access and are ideal for funds you need for daily transactions or active trading. However, this convenience comes with increased risk, as they are more susceptible to online threats. On the other hand, cold storage involves keeping your funds offline, as with hardware or paper wallets. This method is best for long-term storage, where you do not need frequent access to your cryptocurrencies. It ensures maximum security by keeping your assets away from potential online threats.

Choosing the right wallet and implementing robust security practices can protect your digital assets from various threats. Understanding these foundational elements will empower you to manage your investments confidently and securely as you navigate cryptocurrency.

2.3 SECURITY MEASURES: PROTECTING YOUR DIGITAL ASSETS

You may have heard stories of individuals losing all their cryptocurrency investments to cyber-attacks. These incidents underscore the importance of understanding common security threats in the crypto space. Phishing attacks, for instance, are a prevalent risk. They often manifest through deceptive emails or websites that mimic legitimate services, tricking you into revealing sensitive information such as your wallet credentials or private keys. If you're not vigilant, a single click can lead to the theft of your digital assets.

Malware and ransomware pose another significant threat. These malicious programs can infiltrate your device, granting attackers unauthorized access to your private information and cryptocurrency holdings. Ransomware, in particular, can lock you out of your system, demanding payment in digital currency to restore access.

To safeguard your assets, adopting best security practices is non-negotiable. Start by using strong, unique passwords for your wallet and exchange accounts. Avoid the common pitfall of reusing passwords across multiple platforms, as this can create vulnerabilities. Password managers can help you generate and store complex passwords securely. Regularly updating your software is another critical step. Developers frequently release updates to patch security vulnerabilities, so keeping your applications current can protect against the latest threats. Consider enabling automatic updates where possible to ensure you're always protected. Furthermore, be cautious when downloading software or clicking on links, as these can be avenues for malware distribution. Stick to official websites and verified sources to minimize risks.

The security of your private keys is paramount. These keys are your access codes to your cryptocurrency, akin to a PIN for your bank account. Without them, you cannot access or manage your funds. Therefore, you must store your private keys securely to prevent unauthorized access.

Advanced security options are available for those seeking enhanced protection. Multi-signature wallets provide an added layer of security by requiring multiple signatures from different devices before a transaction is authorized. This means that even if one of your devices is compromised, an attacker still needs access to additional devices to complete a transaction. Hardware security modules (HSMs) offer another robust option. These are physical devices that manage digital keys and provide cryptographic operations, ensuring that your private keys remain secure even in the event of a breach. While these advanced options require a deeper understanding and potentially more resources, they offer peace of mind for those managing significant cryptocurrency holdings.

In the ever-evolving digital finance landscape, staying informed and proactive about security is crucial. By understanding the threats and implementing these protective measures, you can secure your assets against potential vulnerabilities and confidently navigate the cryptocurrency world.

2.4 REGULATORY CONSIDERATIONS: WHAT BEGINNERS NEED TO KNOW

Understanding the regulatory landscape is crucial as you step into the cryptocurrency world. Unlike traditional financial systems, cryptocurrencies operate in a largely decentralized environment, which presents unique regulatory challenges. Around the globe, countries differ significantly in their approaches to cryptocurrency regulation. Some nations embrace digital currencies, creating frameworks encouraging innovation while ensuring consumer protection. For instance, in the United States, regulatory bodies such as the Securities and Exchange Commission (SEC) and the Commodity Futures Trading Commission (CFTC) play pivotal roles in overseeing cryptocurrency activities. They ensure that these activities comply with existing financial laws and that investor interests are safeguarded. Meanwhile, countries like China have taken a more restrictive stance, imposing stringent regulations or outright bans on cryptocurrency trading. Such differences underscore the importance of understanding the country's regulatory environment where you intend to engage in cryptocurrency activities.

These regulations impact how cryptocurrencies are traded and exchanged. One of the key regulatory measures is the Know Your Customer (KYC) requirement. This mandates that exchanges verify the identity of their users before allowing them to trade. It's a measure designed to prevent illegal activities such as money laundering and fraud. By requiring valid identification, exchanges can ensure their platforms are not used for illicit purposes. Anti-money laundering (AML) policies further reinforce this by establishing procedures to detect and report suspicious activities. While sometimes seen as hurdles, these regulations are crucial for maintaining the financial system's integrity. They help build trust with users, who can trade knowing that a regulated environment protects them. Understanding KYC and AML policies is vital for beginners as they will encounter these requirements when setting up accounts on most exchanges.

Compliance with these regulations is not just a legal obligation; it's also a safeguard for you as a trader. Adhering to regulatory standards helps avoid legal issues arising from non-compliance, such as fines or account freezes. More importantly, it ensures the legitimacy of your transactions, providing peace of mind that legal authorities protect and recognize your investments. This legitimacy is crucial for gaining the trust of other market participants, making it easier to engage in transactions and partnerships. Additionally, compliance enhances the cryptocurrency market's credibility, encouraging wider adoption and acceptance. As a beginner, aligning with regulatory standards is integral to building a trustworthy and sustainable trading practice.

Staying informed about regulatory changes is essential in the fast-evolving cryptocurrency landscape. Governments and regulatory bodies continuously adapt policies to address emerging challenges and opportunities. To keep abreast of these developments, consider regularly visiting government websites where regulatory updates are often published. These sources provide direct information from the authorities responsible for enforcing the laws. Industry news outlets are another valuable resource. Websites like CoinDesk and CoinTelegraph offer insights into regulatory changes and expert analyses and opinions. They often cover global perspectives, giving a broader understanding of how different regions approach cryptocurrency regulation. Engaging with these resources enables you to anticipate changes that may affect your trading activities, allowing you to adjust your strategies accordingly. As a beginner, cultivating the habit of staying informed will equip you with the knowledge needed to navigate the complexities of the regulatory landscape confidently and effectively.

2.5 AVOIDING SCAMS: IDENTIFYING RED FLAGS

Imagine being approached with an investment opportunity promising high returns that seem too good to be true. This is often the first sign of a Ponzi scheme, a type of scam where returns are paid to earlier investors using the capital from new investors rather than from profit earned. These schemes eventually collapse when the influx of new investors slows down, leaving many without their initial investment. In crypto, Ponzi schemes can present themselves as new digital currencies or platforms that guarantee substantial returns with little risk. It's a red flag when an investment opportunity is shrouded in secrecy, lacking transparency about how profits are generated. If the details of the investment process are unclear or overly complex without justification, it's wise to proceed with caution.

Fake Initial Coin Offerings (ICOs) are another prevalent scam that has ensnared even savvy investors. These scams involve launching a new cryptocurrency project, often accompanied by a slick website and compelling whitepaper, to lure investors under the guise of a legitimate ICO. However, once the funds are raised, the project and the investors' money disappear. To identify such scams, look for clear signs of legitimacy: Does the project have credible developers or advisors with verifiable track records? Are there realistic goals and a clear roadmap available for scrutiny? A lack of transparency in any of these areas should raise suspicion.

Performing due diligence is your best defense against falling victim to scams. Thoroughly researching potential investments involves vetting the project team and investigating their professional backgrounds. Do they have a history of successful projects, or are they new to the industry? Transparency about the team's identity and credentials is crucial. Furthermore, scrutinize the business model. Does it make sense within the market context, and is it feasible? A solid business model should be well-documented and able to withstand critical examination. If the business relies on vague promises of future success without concrete plans or explanations, it may be prudent to steer clear.

Real-world examples highlight the consequences of ignoring these red flags. Take the infamous case of BitConnect, which promised high returns through a lending program that was a classic Ponzi scheme. When the platform collapsed, investors lost millions, and the aftermath served as a stark reminder of the importance of skepticism and due diligence. Another example is the PlexCoin ICO, halted by the U.S. Securities and Exchange Commission (SEC) due to false claims and misleading information, resulting in hefty fines for its founders. These cases illustrate scams' devastating financial and emotional impact on those who fall prey to them.

Understanding and identifying scams is crucial in the cryptocurrency space. As the market grows, so do the opportunities for malicious actors to exploit unsuspecting investors. By staying informed, conducting thorough research, and approaching opportunities with a critical eye, you can protect yourself and your investments from becoming another cautionary tale in the crypto world.

2.6 THE ROLE OF FIAT IN THE WORLD OF CRYPTOCURRENCY

Fiat currency is a crucial bridge to the crypto realm in digital currencies. Fiat currencies, such as the U.S. dollar or the euro, are the foundation for most crypto transactions. They provide a familiar starting point for those venturing into crypto, acting as a gateway. These fiat gateways are platforms where you can convert traditional currency into cryptocurrency. For example, exchanges like Coinbase or Kraken allow you to deposit fiat money from your bank account, which you can use to purchase digital currencies. This conversion is not only convenient but also necessary for those who are new to the crypto ecosystem and are beginning their investment journey. However, the interaction between fiat and crypto is not without its challenges. Exchange rate fluctuations can significantly impact the value of your investments. Since cryptocurrencies are traded against fiat currencies, their value is susceptible to changes in the global currency markets. This volatility can either enhance or diminish your purchasing power, making monitoring exchange rates closely imperative when making transactions.

Fiat currencies remain indispensable in the cryptocurrency trading landscape. They are often the primary means of making initial investments, as most individuals start their crypto experience by purchasing digital assets with fiat money. This initial conversion is a pivotal step, enabling the flow of traditional funds into the decentralized world. Additionally, when it comes time to cash out your crypto profits, fiat currencies are typically the medium through which you convert your digital gains back into spendable cash. This process allows you to realize the financial benefits of your investments tangibly. The utility of fiat in these transactions highlights its enduring relevance, even as digital currencies gain prominence. Without the ability to move quickly between fiat and crypto, users would face significant barriers in accessing the liquidity and flexibility they need for effective trading and investment management.

Stablecoins offer an intriguing alternative to fiat, particularly in their role of mitigating the notorious volatility associated with cryptocurrencies. Unlike traditional digital currencies, stablecoins are designed to maintain a stable value by pegging themselves to assets like fiat currencies. Tether (USDT) and USD Coin (USDC) are among the most popular stablecoins, providing a reliable store of value in the crypto market. These coins facilitate smooth transactions by offering price stability, which is particularly beneficial during market turbulence. For traders, stablecoins serve as a safe haven, allowing them to park their funds without exiting the crypto ecosystem entirely. This stability enables users to manage their portfolios more effectively, reducing the risks associated with price swings and providing a buffer against market shocks.

The relationship between fiat and cryptocurrency is poised for significant evolution. One major development is the emergence of central bank digital currencies (CBDCs). These digital forms of fiat currency, issued by central banks, promise to blend the stability of traditional money with the efficiency of digital transactions. CBDCs could streamline payments, enhance monetary policy implementation, and offer a government-backed alternative to private cryptocurrencies. As countries like China and Sweden test their CBDC initiatives, the potential for widespread adoption grows. Moreover, traditional financial institutions' increasing acceptance of cryptocurrencies marks another pivotal shift. Banks and financial firms are beginning to explore ways to integrate digital assets into their offerings, recognizing the demand and potential for growth in this sector. This integration could create a more seamless coexistence between fiat and cryptocurrencies, fostering a more interconnected and versatile financial landscape.

As we conclude this chapter, it's clear that while cryptocurrencies offer innovative solutions and new opportunities, fiat currencies remain vital to this ecosystem. Their role as a bridge, a stabilizer, and a medium of exchange ensures that both fiat and crypto will continue to coexist, complementing each other in the evolving financial landscape. The next chapter will explore the intricacies of buying and selling cryptocurrency, delving into strategies and practices to help you make informed and strategic decisions.

CHAPTER 3
BUYING AND SELLING CRYPTOCURRENCY

I magine you're at a bustling farmers' market, eager to purchase fresh produce. You notice the prices of vegetables seem to fluctuate wildly throughout the day. This unpredictability mirrors the cryptocurrency market's volatility, where prices rise and fall rapidly. Many newcomers to cryptocurrency are captivated by the potential for profit but are unsure how to enter the market without risking their savings. This chapter guides you through the essentials of investing wisely, ensuring you can participate in the market while maintaining financial security.

3.1 CREATING A SMART CRYPTOCURRENCY INVESTMENT BUDGET

Setting a realistic budget is one of the first steps in investing in cryptocurrency. Understanding your finances is crucial to determining how much you can afford to invest. Start by assessing your disposable income—the available funds after paying for necessary expenses. This includes rent, utilities, groceries, and other essential costs. Once you have a clear picture of your disposable income, you can allocate a portion to invest in cryptocurrencies. It's important to remember that investing should not compromise your financial stability. Only allocate funds you can afford to lose, as the crypto market is notoriously volatile.

A practical strategy to mitigate the risks of investing in a volatile market is dollar-cost averaging. This approach involves making regular, fixed investments in cryptocurrency, regardless of the market's ups and downs. Investing a set amount at consistent intervals reduces the impact of market fluctuations on your portfolio. Over time, this strategy averages out the cost of your investments, potentially smoothing out the highs and lows of market volatility. Dollar-cost averaging encourages a long-term perspective, helping you to focus on gradual growth rather than short-term gains. This method particularly benefits beginners, removing the pressure of timing the market and fostering a disciplined investment habit.

Before diving into cryptocurrency, it's sensible to establish a solid financial foundation by creating an emergency fund. This fund is a financial safety net, covering three to six months of living expenses in case of unforeseen circumstances, such as job loss or medical emergencies. An emergency fund ensures you won't need to dip into your investments during challenging times, allowing your cryptocurrency portfolio to grow uninterrupted. The security of knowing you have a financial cushion can also reduce stress, enabling you to make more rational investment decisions rather than acting out of necessity or fear.

Risk management is another critical component of successful cryptocurrency investing. Diversifying your investments is a fundamental strategy to minimize risk. By spreading your investments across various cryptocurrencies, you reduce the impact of any single asset's poor performance on your overall portfolio. This approach mitigates potential losses and increases the chances of benefiting from different market opportunities. It's also advisable to avoid using leverage, which involves borrowing funds to invest. While leverage can amplify gains, it also magnifies losses, posing a significant risk to your financial health. Keeping your investments simple and within your means is a prudent approach that protects you from the unpredictability of the crypto market.

Personal Finance Checklist

- Assess Disposable Income: Calculate your income after essentials and allocate a portion for investment.
- Establish an Emergency Fund: Secure three to six months of expenses to guard against unexpected events.
- Implement Dollar-Cost Averaging: Set a regular investment schedule to average out market volatility.
- Diversify Investments: Spread your funds across different cryptocurrencies to minimize risk.
- Avoid Leverage: Only invest what you can afford to lose without borrowing additional funds.

By following these guidelines, you can confidently approach cryptocurrency investing, knowing you have taken steps to safeguard your finances while exploring the potential of digital assets.

3.2 STEP-BY-STEP GUIDE TO BUYING YOUR FIRST CRYPTOCURRENCY

When considering your first cryptocurrency purchase, the selection process begins with understanding your purchase. Start by examining the market capitalization of the cryptocurrency. Market cap is a straightforward metric: it represents the total value of a cryptocurrency by multiplying its current price by the total supply of coins. A higher market cap often indicates a more stable and established cryptocurrency. This can be an essential factor in your decision-making, as it reflects the level of trust and adoption in the market. Equally important is the use case and technology behind the cryptocurrency. Some coins, like Bitcoin, act as a digital store of value, while others, like Ethereum, provide a platform for decentralized applications. Understanding the purpose and functionality of a cryptocurrency helps you align your investment with your expectations and goals.

Once you've decided on a cryptocurrency, the purchasing process begins with setting up an account on a cryptocurrency exchange. Choose a reputable exchange that aligns with your needs, considering factors like ease of use, security features, and supported currencies. Begin by visiting the exchange's website and clicking on the registration link. You'll need to provide your email address and create a strong password. After registering, the next step is identity verification. Exchanges require this to comply with regulations and ensure the security of their platforms. This process typically involves submitting a government-issued ID and possibly a selfie for identity confirmation. Once your identity is verified, you can fund your account using fiat currency. With your account ready, navigate to the trading section of the exchange and search for the cryptocurrency you wish to buy. Placing a buy order is straightforward: specify the amount you want to purchase and confirm the transaction. The exchange will execute your order based on the current market price, and the cryptocurrency will appear in your account balance.

As you venture into cryptocurrency transactions, ensuring their security is paramount. One of the most effective ways to protect your account is by enabling two-factor authentication (2FA). This security measure requires your password and a second piece of information, typically a code sent to your mobile device, to access your account. This added layer of security significantly reduces the risk of unauthorized access. Additionally, transactions should always be conducted over secure networks. Avoid using public Wi-Fi when accessing your cryptocurrency accounts, as these networks can be vulnerable to hacking. Instead, opt for a private, secure internet connection to safeguard sensitive information. By taking these precautions, you can minimize the risk of cyber threats and ensure your transactions remain safe.

3.3 TRANSFERRING YOUR CRYPTOCURRENCY TO YOUR WALLET

After purchasing cryptocurrency, the next step is to store it securely. While exchanges offer convenience with built-in wallets, they are not the safest option for long-term storage due to potential vulnerabilities. Transferring your cryptocurrency to a personal wallet is a recommended practice. As explained in the previous section, wallets come in two main types: hot and cold.

Initially, transferring a small amount of cryptocurrency from an exchange to your personal wallet is an essential step for several reasons. It allows you to verify the transfer process to ensure it works smoothly, including ensuring you have correctly set up your wallet address and can successfully receive funds. Cryptocurrency transactions are irreversible. If you make an error in the wallet address or use an incorrect network (e.g., sending tokens to a wrong blockchain), a small test transaction helps catch these errors before you risk more significant amounts.

When you transfer to your wallet, the private key controls access to your funds. You want to ensure your wallet is adequately secured and that you have access to it. This test allows you to confirm that you can access your funds and that your security measures (e.g., two-factor authentication, backup phrase) are in place. If you plan to store cryptocurrency in a hardware wallet (cold storage), the test transaction will help ensure you can access and manage your funds on that device.

Cryptocurrency transfers can incur fees depending on the network and the transaction size. By testing with a small amount, you can better understand the costs and plan for future larger transfers.

Different exchanges have varying withdrawal speeds, and the blockchain networks can also differ in how quickly they process transactions. A small test transfer will indicate how long it will take for funds to be successfully sent to your wallet and provide reassurance that the exchange's withdrawal function works correctly.

In conclusion, performing a test transfer with a small amount of cryptocurrency allows you to check the functionality of your wallet and exchange, confirm the correct address and network compatibility, and ensure your security measures are working correctly. This step helps minimize the risks of losing considerable amounts of cryptocurrency due to human error or technical issues.

3.4 SELLING CRYPTOCURRENCY: TIMING AND STRATEGIES

Selling cryptocurrency is a critical part of your investment strategy, and timing your sale is as important as when you first decide to buy. Understanding when to sell is crucial for maximizing your returns, as it demands a keen awareness of market conditions and a strong understanding of market trends and behaviors. The first step is to analyze historical price movements. Reviewing past performance lets you identify patterns or cycles that might repeat, helping you anticipate potential price movements. For example, periods of rapid growth are often followed by corrections, which could indicate that the asset is overbought and might be due for a decline. To better gauge the market's momentum, consider using technical indicators, such as moving averages and the Relative Strength Index (RSI). These tools help assess whether a cryptocurrency is in a strong uptrend (and may still have room to grow) or if it is overvalued (and could soon experience a drop). In addition to technical analysis, staying informed about current news and market sentiment is crucial. News of regulatory changes, technological advancements, or macroeconomic events can trigger significant price shifts in the market, and these factors can often provide timely clues for selling. By combining both technical and fundamental analysis, you can make more informed decisions about when to sell your cryptocurrency holdings.

Depending on your financial goals and risk tolerance, you can employ various strategies when selling cryptocurrency. One common approach is profit-taking, which involves selling portions of your holdings as the value increases. This strategy helps secure some profits while still leaving room for further appreciation. For instance, if you purchased a cryptocurrency at a lower price and it increases by 30%, you could sell a small percentage of your position. As the price continues to rise, you could sell additional portions incrementally. This way, you lock in gains along the way and avoid the risk of holding everything until a market correction happens. In volatile markets, where prices fluctuate wildly, this approach helps you avoid the temptation to make emotional, hasty decisions and protects you from dramatic downturns. Another helpful strategy is setting up stop-loss orders. These orders automatically trigger a sale when the price drops to a certain level, helping protect your investments from more significant losses. By setting a predetermined price point to exit a position, you avoid the need for constant monitoring and reduce the risk of selling too late when the market has already declined significantly. Both profit-taking and stop-loss strategies are highly effective but require thoughtful planning and a clear understanding of your risk tolerance. The more you practice these strategies, the better you'll manage risk and stay disciplined in your approach.

It's also important to recognize that the psychological aspects of selling can majorly impact your decisions. Fear and greed are powerful emotions when investing, often leading to impulsive actions. For example, fear might prompt you to panic sell during a market downturn, cutting your losses prematurely. On the other hand, greed may cause you to hold onto an asset for too long, hoping for further gains, only to see the value decline. To combat these emotional responses, it's vital to establish predefined exit points before entering a trade. Regardless of short-term market fluctuations, setting clear goals for when and how much you plan to sell helps you maintain discipline and stick to your strategy. Creating a plan reduces the influence of emotions like fear and greed, ensuring that your decisions remain rational and aligned with your long-term financial objectives. Remember, cryptocurrency markets are cyclical, and temporary downturns are a normal part of the process. Staying calm, adhering to your plan, and not making impulsive decisions are key to successfully navigating the ups and downs of the market.

To illustrate the effectiveness of these strategies, let's consider the example of Emily, an investor who applied a disciplined profit-taking strategy. Emily initially purchased a well-known cryptocurrency at a relatively low price, anticipating future growth. As the value of her investment increased over time, she resisted the urge to sell everything at once. Instead, she decided to sell 20% of her holdings each time the price increased by 25%. This incremental approach allowed her to lock in profits while still benefiting from potential further price appreciation. By selling her final portion, Emily had realized substantial gains, far exceeding her initial investment. Her strategy of taking profits gradually while still allowing her remaining holdings to grow highlights the power of patience and planning in a volatile market. It also demonstrates how a well-executed strategy can result in better financial outcomes.

To successfully implement these strategies, it's essential to recognize that selling cryptocurrency requires patience and practice. Understanding market conditions, setting clear goals, and controlling your emotions are all key factors contributing to effective selling. Over time, as you develop a deeper understanding of the market, you'll gain confidence in your ability to make informed and strategic decisions that align with your long-term investment objectives. The more you practice and hone these techniques, the better prepared you'll be to navigate the complexities of the cryptocurrency market and reach your financial objectives.

3.5 UNDERSTANDING TRANSACTION FEES AND COSTS

Navigating the cryptocurrency market involves more than just buying and selling; it's crucial to understand the fees associated with these transactions. Every exchange has its fee structure, which can significantly affect your profitability. Trading fees are the most common, typically charged as a percentage of the transaction amount. Depending on your trading volume or membership level, they can vary between exchanges and even within the same platform. For instance, high-frequency traders might benefit from lower fees due to their substantial market activity. Withdrawal fees are another cost to consider. You'll likely incur a fee once you move your cryptocurrency from an exchange to a personal wallet. This charge can fluctuate based on the specific currency and the current market conditions. Network fees, sometimes called mining fees, are also a factor. These are paid to miners or validators to process your transaction on the blockchain. The fee amount often depends on network congestion; the busier the network, the higher the fee. Understanding these fees is vital, as they can add up and eat into your potential gains.

The impact of these fees on your overall profitability is significant. When planning trades, it's essential to calculate net gains, considering all associated costs. For example, if you buy a cryptocurrency at a specific price and it appreciates, you might assume a straightforward profit. However, once you factor in trading fees, withdrawal fees, and network costs, your actual profit could be considerably less. This is why careful planning is crucial. Before executing a trade, simulate the entire process and account for every potential fee. This way, you can make informed decisions that align with your financial goals. Ignoring fees can lead to unexpected costs, turning what seemed like a profitable venture into a less favorable outcome.

Minimizing transaction costs can bolster your bottom line. One strategy is to compare exchange rates across different platforms. While it might seem convenient to stick with one exchange, exploring alternatives can reveal lower fees or better rates, potentially saving you significant amounts over time. Additionally, timing your transactions during low network congestion can reduce network fees. Blockchain networks experience varying levels of activity throughout the day. By executing your transactions during off-peak times, you might enjoy reduced fees. This requires patience and planning, but the savings can be worthwhile, especially for frequent traders.

Popular exchanges employ different fee structures that can influence your trading strategy. Many platforms use tiered fee structures, where the fee percentage decreases as your trading volume increases over a specified period. This model rewards active traders but might not benefit those who trade infrequently. Another common model is the maker-taker fee structure. In this system, "makers," who provide liquidity by placing limit orders, often pay lower fees than "takers," who consume liquidity by executing market orders. Understanding which category you fall into can help you optimize your trades for lower costs. For instance, if you frequently place market orders, consider adjusting your strategy to take advantage of lower maker fees.

Crypto Fee Checklist

- Trading Fees: Check exchange fee percentages and how they vary with trading volume.
- Withdrawal Fees: Understand the costs associated with transferring funds to a wallet.
- Network Fees: Monitor network congestion to time transactions for lower fees.
- Exchange Rates: Compare rates across multiple platforms to find the most cost-effective option.
- Fee Structures: Familiarize yourself with tiered and maker-taker models to strategize accordingly.

Through awareness and strategic planning, you can navigate the complexities of transaction fees, ensuring that your investment decisions are informed and financially rewarding.

3.6 TAX IMPLICATIONS: NAVIGATING THE LEGAL ASPECTS

Understanding the tax implications of cryptocurrency is crucial for any investor. Tax authorities like the Internal Revenue Service (IRS) in the United States treat cryptocurrencies as property. When you sell or trade cryptocurrency, you may be liable for capital gains tax. This tax applies to the profit you make from selling your digital assets. If you hold the cryptocurrency for more than a year before selling, it qualifies for long-term capital gains tax, which typically has a lower rate than short-term gains, applicable to assets held for less than a year. Income tax considerations also come into play when you receive cryptocurrency as payment for goods or services. These transactions are treated as ordinary income, and the cryptocurrency's fair market value at the time of receipt is included in your gross income. Being aware of these distinctions helps you plan your investments and transactions with an understanding of the potential tax liabilities.

Keeping meticulous records of your cryptocurrency transactions is not just advisable; it's necessary. Accurate record-keeping ensures you can correctly report your gains and losses during tax submissions. Begin by tracking the purchase prices of your cryptocurrencies, as this information is critical for calculating capital gains or losses. Note the date of each transaction, the amount of cryptocurrency bought or sold, and its value in fiat currency at the time. This level of detail is essential for accurate tax reporting. Many investors use spreadsheets or specialized software to maintain these records, ensuring that every transaction is accounted for. Having detailed records not only facilitates tax compliance but also helps in optimizing your tax strategy.

When it comes to reporting cryptocurrency on your tax returns, accuracy is paramount. Tax software can be invaluable, offering a streamlined way to track transactions and calculate gains or losses. These programs can often import transaction data directly from exchanges, simplifying the reporting process. Consulting a tax professional with experience in digital assets is also a wise step. They can provide guidance on complex issues, such as the implications of crypto-to-crypto trades, which are taxable events despite not involving fiat currency. A professional can also help you claim any available deductions or credits that can significantly affect your overall tax liability.

Speaking of deductions, it's worth exploring potential tax deductions and credits that might apply to your cryptocurrency activities. One such opportunity is the ability to offset capital losses against capital gains. You can use this loss to reduce your taxable gains if you've sold cryptocurrency for less than you paid. If your losses exceed your gains, you may be able to deduct the remaining amount, up to a specific limit, from your other income. This can provide significant tax relief, especially in volatile markets with substantial losses. Additionally, charitable donations made in cryptocurrency are eligible for tax deductions, offering another potential benefit. Donating appreciated cryptocurrency can also allow you to avoid capital gains tax on the appreciation, making it a tax-efficient way to contribute to causes you care about.

Navigating the tax landscape of cryptocurrency requires diligence and an informed approach. It's not just about compliance; it's about understanding how tax laws affect your investment strategy and leveraging that knowledge to make informed decisions. By maintaining detailed records, seeking professional guidance, and exploring opportunities for deductions, you can manage your tax obligations effectively while maximizing your investment potential.

3.7 HOW TO AVOID COMMON MISTAKES WHEN TRADING

Entering the cryptocurrency trading world can be exhilarating, yet it is fraught with potential pitfalls. Among the most common mistakes new traders make is chasing losses—a behavior driven by the desire to recoup money lost in previous trades. This often leads to impulsive decisions and increased risk-taking, exacerbating the initial loss rather than recovering it. Maintain a clear head and remember that not every trade will be a winner. Accepting losses as part of the trading experience allows you to move forward strategically rather than emotionally.

Another frequent error is overtrading, a scenario where traders execute too many trades in a short period, often based on short-term market fluctuations rather than a coherent strategy. Overtrading can deplete your capital quickly due to transaction fees and poorly timed trades. It also increases stress and the likelihood of making decisions driven by emotion rather than logic. To counteract this, establish a trading plan outlining specific criteria for entering and exiting trades. This plan should be based on thorough research and market analysis, ensuring that each trade is a calculated decision rather than a reaction to market noise.

Research and due diligence form the backbone of informed decision-making in cryptocurrency trading. Analyzing market data is essential, providing insights into trends and potential turning points. Stay updated with the latest news, as regulation, technology, or global economic developments can impact cryptocurrency prices. A well-informed trader is better equipped to anticipate market movements and make strategic decisions. Regularly reviewing credible sources and engaging with the community can enhance your understanding and keep you abreast of emerging trends. This ongoing education aids in refining your strategies and adapting to the ever-changing market landscape.

Discipline in trading is cultivated through setting clear goals and adhering to a structured plan. Define what you hope to achieve with your trading activities, whether it be short-term gains or long-term growth. These goals will guide your strategy and provide a benchmark for measuring success. Sticking to your plan involves resisting the temptation to deviate based on short-term market fluctuations. By maintaining consistency, you build a track record that helps you evaluate what works and what doesn't, allowing for gradual improvement and refinement of your approach. This disciplined mindset is crucial for navigating the volatile nature of cryptocurrency markets.

Consider the experience of a trader named Jake, who learned valuable lessons through trial and error. Initially, Jake succumbed to chasing losses, making hasty decisions that led to further financial setbacks. Realizing the unsustainable nature of this approach, he decided to step back and reassess his strategy. Jake began implementing a disciplined approach, setting clear entry and exit points for each trade, backed by thorough research. Over time, his results improved significantly, demonstrating the power of a strategic, well-reasoned approach to trading. Jake's story serves as a reminder that while mistakes are inevitable, they can be valuable learning tools to inform future decisions.

As you continue to explore the world of cryptocurrency trading, remember that mistakes are part of the learning process. By recognizing common errors and implementing strategies to avoid them, you can enhance your trading experience and improve your outcomes. With research, discipline, and a willingness to adapt, you can navigate the complexities of the market with increased confidence and competence. As we move into the next chapter, we'll explore how to safeguard your investments, ensuring that your trading activities are profitable, secure, and sustainable.

CHAPTER 4
SAFEGUARDING YOUR INVESTMENTS

Picture yourself standing at the edge of a sprawling forest, each tree representing a different investment opportunity. The forest is vast, filled with towering oaks and delicate saplings, each offering its own potential for growth. As you navigate this landscape, the path to financial security lies not in betting everything on a single tree but in cultivating a diverse array of investments. This is the essence of diversification—a strategy that spreads your investments across various assets to mitigate risk and enhance the potential for steady returns. Understanding and implementing diversification is crucial for newcomers to cryptocurrency, as it reduces exposure to the volatility of any single asset and balances the inherent risks and rewards within your portfolio.

4.1 THE POWER OF DIVERSIFICATION IN CRYPTOCURRENCY INVESTING

Diversification is a cornerstone of prudent investing because it minimizes the impact of poor performance by any one investment on your overall portfolio. By reducing your exposure to a single asset, you safeguard against the unpredictable nature of the cryptocurrency market, where prices can fluctuate wildly in short periods. This approach allows you to balance high-risk investments with more stable ones, creating a buffer to protect your assets during market downturns. Think of it as spreading your eggs across multiple baskets—if one basket falls, the others remain intact, preserving your wealth.

The cryptocurrency market offers diverse asset classes, each with unique characteristics and potential. Large-cap cryptocurrencies like Bitcoin and Ethereum are akin to the sturdy oaks of our forest—established, reliable, and widely recognized. These assets often serve as the foundation of a diversified portfolio due to their stability and liquidity. In contrast, small-cap cryptocurrencies represent emerging opportunities akin to the young saplings with the potential for significant growth. While they carry higher risk, they also offer the possibility of substantial returns. Beyond these categories, the market includes utility tokens, which provide access to specific services or products, and security tokens, representing ownership in an asset or company. Each type of token serves a different purpose and can contribute to a well-rounded investment strategy.

To effectively diversify within the crypto market, consider allocating percentages of your portfolio to different types of assets. This might involve investing a substantial portion in large-cap cryptocurrencies for stability while dedicating smaller amounts to small-cap options with higher growth potential. Additionally, mixing established cryptocurrencies with emerging ones allows you to capitalize on both reliability and innovation. Regularly reassessing and rebalancing your portfolio ensures it aligns with your evolving investment goals and risk tolerance. By doing so, you maintain a dynamic approach that adapts to market changes and personal circumstances.

The long-term benefits of diversification are significant, offering a smoother investment journey and increased stability of returns. This strategy helps mitigate the effects of market volatility, as gains in one area can offset losses in another, leading to a more consistent performance over time. A diversified portfolio makes you less likely to experience dramatic swings in value, providing peace of mind and financial security. Moreover, diversification encourages a broader understanding of cryptocurrency as you engage with different assets and explore their unique roles and potential. This knowledge enhances your investment acumen and empowers you to make informed decisions that align with your financial aspirations.

Diversification Planning Exercise

To help you apply these principles, consider undertaking a diversification planning exercise. Begin by listing your current cryptocurrency holdings and noting each asset's percentage in your portfolio. Next, categorize these assets by type, such as large-cap, small-cap, utility, and security tokens. Reflect on your risk tolerance and investment goals, then adjust your allocations to ensure a balanced mix. This exercise clarifies your current strategy and highlights potential growth and improvement areas.

This chapter explored how diversification can safeguard investments by spreading risk and enhancing stability. By embracing this strategy, you can build a resilient portfolio that withstands market fluctuations while seizing growth opportunities.

4.2 RISK MANAGEMENT: PROTECTING YOUR INVESTMENTS

Engaging with cryptocurrency markets requires a keen awareness of the inherent risks that can impact your investments. One of the most significant threats is the potential for security breaches. Unlike traditional financial systems, cryptocurrencies are susceptible to hacking attempts due to their digital nature. Cybercriminals target exchanges and wallets, seeking vulnerabilities to exploit. A single security lapse can result in substantial financial losses, as hackers may access your digital assets illegally. This risk underscores the importance of robust security practices and choosing reputable platforms with proven security measures to protect your holdings.

Market volatility is another challenge that cryptocurrency investors face. The prices of digital currencies can fluctuate dramatically within short periods, influenced by factors such as market sentiment, technological advancements, and geopolitical events. This volatility can present profit opportunities but also risk significant losses. Investors must be prepared for sudden price swings and develop strategies to manage these fluctuations effectively. Understanding the market dynamics and staying informed about current events can help mitigate the impact of volatility on your investments.

Regulatory changes further complicate the landscape of cryptocurrency investing. Governments worldwide continuously adapt and enforce regulations to keep pace with the evolving digital asset market. These changes can affect cryptocurrencies' legality, taxation, and operational aspects, influencing their value and usability. For investors, staying abreast of regulatory developments is crucial, as new laws can impact investment strategies and trading activities. Monitoring reliable news sources and regulatory updates can provide valuable insights into potential changes in the legal environment, helping you make informed decisions.

To effectively assess these risks, employing risk assessment techniques is vital. Conducting a SWOT analysis—evaluating strengths, weaknesses, opportunities, and threats—can provide a comprehensive view of your investment landscape. This analysis helps identify vulnerability and potential growth areas, guiding you in making informed decisions. Using risk assessment tools, such as scenario analysis and stress testing, can further refine your understanding of how different factors may impact your investments. These techniques allow you to simulate various scenarios and gauge their potential effects on your portfolio, enhancing your ability to anticipate and respond to challenges.

Mitigating risks involves implementing strategies that can safeguard your investments. Setting stop-loss orders is a practical step to protect against unexpected market downturns. These orders automatically sell your holdings when their price falls to a predetermined level, limiting potential losses. This strategy allows you to manage risk without actively monitoring the market at all times. Additionally, using hedging strategies, such as diversifying into stablecoins or other asset classes, can provide a buffer against volatility. Hedging involves taking positions that offset potential losses in your primary investments, ensuring stability and preserving capital during turbulent times.

Understanding your risk tolerance is a fundamental aspect of risk management. Each investor has a unique capacity for handling risk, influenced by financial goals, investment horizon, and personal comfort with uncertainty. Self-assessment questionnaires can help you determine your risk tolerance level by evaluating your reaction to hypothetical investment scenarios. These assessments provide a clearer picture of your risk appetite, enabling you to align your investment strategies accordingly. Ensuring your portfolio reflects your risk tolerance is crucial, as this alignment reduces stress and supports sound decision-making.

Risk management in cryptocurrency investing involves identifying, assessing, and mitigating potential investment threats. By understanding the key risks, employing effective assessment techniques, and implementing protective strategies, you can navigate the digital asset market with greater confidence and resilience.

4.3 KEEPING EMOTIONS IN CHECK: TRADING WITH DISCIPLINE

In the trading world, emotions can be a trader's best guide and their worst enemy. The cryptocurrency market often evokes intense feelings with its rapid fluctuations and high stakes. Fear and greed are two dominant emotions that traders commonly experience. Fear can cause panic selling, where investors hastily sell off their assets during a market downturn, often at a loss. This reaction is driven by the fear of losing everything, leading to decisions that may not align with long-term strategies.

On the other hand, greed can drive traders to hold onto assets longer than they should, hoping for further gains. Which often results in missing out on opportunities to secure profits. These cycles of fear and greed create a volatile trading environment where emotional decision-making can lead to costly mistakes.

Managing emotions while trading requires deliberate practice and self-awareness. Taking a moment to breathe and reflect before deciding can prevent hasty actions driven by fear or greed. Setting predetermined trading rules is another effective strategy. By establishing criteria for entering and exiting trades ahead of time, traders can reduce the influence of emotions on their decisions. These rules guide traders, helping them stick to their plans even when the market becomes unpredictable.

Discipline is the backbone of successful trading. It requires consistency and the ability to adhere to a well-defined trading plan. A disciplined approach involves setting clear objectives and following a structured strategy, regardless of market conditions. This consistency helps traders avoid impulsive decisions arising from emotional responses to short-term price fluctuations. By committing to a trading plan, traders develop a sense of control over their actions, which can lead to more favorable outcomes. Avoiding impulsive decisions means resisting the temptation to react to every market movement. Instead, traders should focus on their long-term goals and remain steadfast in their strategies. This discipline fosters a sense of stability, allowing traders to navigate the market with greater confidence.

Consider the cautionary tale of a trader named Mark, who fell victim to the fear of missing out, commonly known as FOMO. Mark learned about a new cryptocurrency skyrocketing in value and became convinced he was on the verge of missing a lucrative opportunity. Overwhelmed by the excitement and the fear of being left behind, he invested a significant portion of his savings into the asset without conducting thorough research. Unfortunately, the bubble burst soon after, and the cryptocurrency's value plummeted, resulting in a substantial loss for Mark. His experience illustrates how emotions, particularly FOMO, can cloud judgment and lead to regrettable decisions. It serves as a reminder of the importance of maintaining composure and making informed choices based on sound analysis rather than emotional impulses.

Trading in the cryptocurrency market demands financial acumen and emotional intelligence. By acknowledging the impact of emotions and adopting strategies to control them, traders can improve their decision-making and increase their likelihood of success. Mindfulness, discipline, and well-defined trading rules are essential tools that empower traders to navigate the complexities of the market with clarity and confidence.

4.4 THE IMPORTANCE OF CONTINUOUS LEARNING AND ADAPTATION

The cryptocurrency market is dynamic, constantly reshaping itself with rapid technological advancements and ever-evolving regulations. This landscape demands that investors stay informed to navigate the complexities and seize opportunities effectively. New technologies emerge regularly, introducing innovative solutions and platforms that can dramatically impact market dynamics. These developments require a keen awareness and willingness to learn, as they can quickly make existing strategies obsolete. Meanwhile, regulatory frameworks are constantly in flux as governments worldwide strive to keep pace with the fast-evolving digital asset ecosystem. These changes can influence everything from legal compliance to market accessibility, making it vital to remain vigilant and informed about local and global regulatory shifts.

Continuous learning is beneficial and necessary to keep up with these changes. Online courses and webinars offer accessible platforms for acquiring up-to-date knowledge and understanding current trends. Many institutions and experts provide these resources, covering various topics catering to beginners and seasoned investors. These courses can provide in-depth insights into new technologies, trading strategies, and regulatory updates. Attending industry conferences and events is another excellent way to stay abreast of the latest developments. These gatherings bring together thought leaders, innovators, and fellow investors, offering opportunities to learn from the best in the field. They also provide a platform for networking, allowing you to connect with like-minded individuals who share your interest in cryptocurrency and can offer valuable perspectives.

Adaptability is a crucial trait for successful investing. The ability to pivot investments based on market conditions can differentiate a thriving portfolio from a stagnant one. As market dynamics shift, so too should your strategies. This might involve reallocating assets, exploring new investment vehicles, or altering risk management practices. For example, reducing exposure and exploring other assets with more stable prospects may be wise if a particular cryptocurrency faces increased regulatory scrutiny. Adaptability also means being open to embracing new technologies and platforms that can enhance your trading efficiency and effectiveness. By staying flexible and willing to evolve, you can better position yourself to capitalize on emerging opportunities while mitigating potential risks.

Proactive learning habits are instrumental in fostering a mindset of growth and adaptability. Setting clear learning goals can guide your educational endeavors, ensuring your efforts align with your investment objectives. For instance, you might set a goal to understand the impact of blockchain technology on specific industries, such as finance or healthcare. These goals provide direction and motivation, helping you prioritize learning activities and track progress. Networking with industry professionals is another powerful tool for expanding your knowledge and gaining fresh insights. Engaging with experts and peers can offer new perspectives, challenge your assumptions, and introduce you to innovative ideas and strategies you might not have considered. Building a network of knowledgeable contacts can also provide support and guidance as you navigate the complexities of the crypto market.

4.5 TOOLS AND RESOURCES FOR STAYING INFORMED

Navigating the cryptocurrency market requires more than intuition; it demands reliable information and data access. One of the most effective ways to stay informed is through cryptocurrency news aggregators. These platforms compile news from various sources, offering a comprehensive view of market trends, regulatory updates, and technological advancements. You can quickly sift through headlines and dive into articles impacting your investment decisions using a news aggregator. This tool saves time and ensures you are always up-to-date with the latest developments in the crypto world. Popular aggregators such as CoinDesk and CoinTelegraph provide timely updates, making them invaluable resources for any investor seeking to remain informed and ahead of the curve.

Portfolio tracking apps are another essential tool for cryptocurrency investors. These applications allow you to monitor your investments in real time, providing insights into the performance of your assets. With features such as price alerts, profit and loss tracking, and historical data analysis, these apps enable you to make informed decisions about buying, selling, or holding your cryptocurrencies. They also offer a consolidated view of all your investments, simplifying managing multiple digital assets. Portfolio trackers like Blockfolio and Delta are widely used for their user-friendly interfaces and comprehensive data analytics. They make them indispensable for investors who wish to stay organized and responsive to market changes.

Data-driven insights are essential for making informed investment decisions, and analytics tools play a key role in delivering these valuable insights. Technical analysis platforms, for instance, offer charts and indicators that help you understand market trends and price movements. You can predict potential future movements and make strategic trading decisions by analyzing patterns such as moving averages and support and resistance levels. On the other hand, Sentiment analysis tools gauge market sentiment by analyzing social media, news outlets, and forums. These tools provide a sense of the overall mood in the market, whether optimistic or pessimistic, allowing you to anticipate potential market shifts. Platforms like CryptoQuant and Coinfeeds.ai offer these analytics, equipping you with the knowledge to navigate the volatile crypto market confidently.

Evaluating the credibility of resources is vital to ensuring that the information you base your decisions on is accurate and reliable. When assessing a source, start by checking the author's credentials. Look for authors with a proven track record in the cryptocurrency industry, as their expertise lends credibility to their insights. Additionally, verify the information by cross-referencing it with multiple sources. This practice confirms the data's accuracy and exposes you to different perspectives, enriching your understanding of the topic. Being discerning about the sources you trust helps protect you from misinformation and ensures that your investment strategies are grounded in factual and well-supported analysis.

Engaging with the cryptocurrency community is another valuable way to enhance your knowledge and stay informed. Participating in online forums allows you to connect with other investors, share insights, and discuss market trends. Platforms like Reddit's r/CryptoCurrency or BitcoinTalk provide spaces for lively discussions and exchanging ideas. These forums are educational and foster a sense of community among crypto enthusiasts. Additionally, joining local meetups can offer opportunities to network with like-minded individuals in your area. These gatherings often feature guest speakers, workshops, and panel discussions, providing firsthand insights into the latest developments in the cryptocurrency world. Engaging with the community keeps you informed and can inspire new investment strategies and approaches.

4.6 CASE STUDIES: LEARNING FROM THE MISTAKES OF OTHERS

In the volatile world of cryptocurrencies, learning from past mistakes is invaluable. Take the infamous BitConnect case, for instance. Promising investors astronomical returns through a lending program, BitConnect operated like a classic Ponzi scheme. It paid early investors the money from new participants rather than actual profits. When the scheme collapsed, many lost their investments, showcasing the dangers of believing in too-good-to-be-true promises. The fallout left a trail of financial ruin and legal battles, highlighting the critical need for due diligence and skepticism in investment decisions.

Another notable example is the 2018 market crash when cryptocurrency values plummeted. Enthusiastic investors who had over-committed during the preceding bull market faced devastating losses. This crash underscored the perils of overexposure to a single asset class, reminding investors that diversification is not just a strategy but a necessity.

Analyzing these cases reveals common threads of oversight and misjudgment. In the BitConnect scenario, many investors failed to perform thorough due diligence. The allure of quick profits drew them in without investigating the project's fundamentals or the feasibility of its promises. A deeper examination might have uncovered red flags, such as the lack of transparency about how returns were generated. Similarly, during the 2018 crash, overexposure to a single asset or market segment left investors vulnerable to severe downturns. This risk could have been mitigated by diversifying holdings across various asset classes, thereby spreading risk and reducing the impact of a single market event. Such analysis emphasizes the importance of informed decision-making based on solid research and a clear understanding of potential risks.

Applying these lessons to your investing approach requires actionable steps. Strengthening your security measures is a fundamental starting point. Use robust, unique passwords for exchange accounts and enable two-factor authentication to protect against unauthorized access. Consider using hardware wallets to store significant holdings, offering enhanced protection against cyber threats. Diversifying your investments is equally crucial. Allocate your portfolio across different cryptocurrencies and asset classes to cushion the impact of market volatility. This strategy spreads risk and positions you to capitalize on varied market opportunities. It's about balancing potential returns and the inherent risks associated with each investment.

Adopting a mindset that views mistakes as opportunities for growth can transform your investment journey. Reflecting on personal missteps allows you to identify patterns of behavior or decision-making that may have led to undesirable outcomes. This reflection fosters self-awareness and encourages the development of more effective strategies. Embracing a growth mindset involves recognizing that errors are not failures but learning experiences. It empowers you to adapt and improve your approach, building resilience and confidence in your investment decisions. This perspective enhances your financial acumen and cultivates a more flexible and adaptive approach to investing.

As we wrap up this chapter on safeguarding your investments, remember that the cornerstone of success lies in learning from your own experiences and those of others. By applying these insights, you can navigate the complexities of the cryptocurrency market with greater assurance and foresight. The next chapter will explore the strategies for developing a smart investment approach that aligns with your goals and risk tolerance, empowering you to make informed choices in the ever-evolving digital finance landscape.

MAKE A DIFFERENCE WITH YOUR REVIEW
UNLOCK THE POWER OF GENEROSITY

"The best way to find yourself is to lose yourself in the service of others."

MAHATMA GANDHI

People who share without expecting anything in return often find happiness in helping others. Let's make a difference together!

Would you help someone like you who is curious about cryptocurrency but unsure where to start?

My goal with *The New Digital Gold: A Simple Guide to Cryptocurrency* is to make learning about digital currency easy, fun, and accessible for everyone.

But to reach more readers, I need your help.

Most people decide to pick up a book based on reviews. By leaving your review, you can help someone else take their first step into the exciting world of cryptocurrency.

It costs nothing, takes less than a minute, and can change someone's journey. Your review could help…

- …one more beginner feel confident exploring cryptocurrency.
- …one more student understand digital currency.

- ...one more investor start their journey with knowledge.

To make a difference, simply scan the QR code below:

If you love helping others, you're my kind of person. Thank you from the bottom of my heart!

Maxwell Westbrook

CHAPTER 5
DEVELOPING A SMART INVESTMENT STRATEGY

Picture a treasure map where X marks the spot of financial success, but the path is not a straight line; it's a series of steps, each representing a carefully set goal. Setting realistic financial goals in cryptocurrency is akin to charting your course on this map. It ensures that your investments align with your broader life objectives, allowing you to measure progress and celebrate success. Without clear goals, investing can feel aimless and chaotic, leaving you vulnerable to market volatility. Establishing these goals anchors your investment strategy, providing a sense of direction and purpose.

5.1 SETTING SMART GOALS FOR CRYPTOCURRENCY INVESTING

The SMART criteria—Specific, Measurable, Achievable, Relevant, and Time-bound—offer a framework for setting practical investment goals. Start by defining specific investment targets. Instead of a vague aim like "make more money," consider a concrete goal such as "grow my crypto portfolio by 20% over the next year." This specificity helps you focus your efforts and track your progress. Measurable goals allow you to quantify your achievements, providing motivation and clarity. Achievability ensures that while your goals are challenging, they remain within reach, preventing discouragement. Ensure your goals are relevant, meaning they align with your values and life aspirations. Finally, setting a time-bound deadline instills urgency, encouraging consistent action and accountability.

Your risk appetite plays a critical role in shaping your financial goals. Assessing your tolerance for risk helps you balance potential rewards against possible setbacks. Some investors thrive on high-stakes ventures, while others prefer a more conservative approach. Reflect on how much risk you're comfortable taking and adjust your goals accordingly. Consider how market conditions might affect your risk tolerance. Adjust your goals to prioritize stability over rapid growth in a volatile market. Conversely, a bullish market might encourage more ambitious objectives. The key is to remain adaptable, allowing your goals to evolve with changing circumstances.

To bring these concepts to life, consider realistic crypto investment goals that cater to different life stages and aspirations. For instance, you might set a goal to save for a significant purchase, such as a down payment on a house. In this case, you could aim to accumulate a specific amount in cryptocurrency over a set period, using it as a supplement to traditional savings. Alternatively, you might focus on building a retirement fund. Here, your goal could involve gradually increasing your crypto holdings with an eye on long-term growth. This approach allows you to harness the potential of digital assets as part of a diversified retirement strategy.

SMART Goal Setting Exercise

- Specific: Define a clear target, such as "Increase my crypto portfolio by 15% in six months."
- Measurable: Track progress with regular portfolio reviews.
- Achievable: Ensure the goal is realistic based on current investment capacity.
- Relevant: Align the goal with broader financial aims, like saving for a vacation.
- Time-bound: Set a completion date to maintain focus and motivation.

Integrating SMART goals into your investment strategy creates a structured approach that enhances decision-making and resilience. This helps navigate the uncertainties of the crypto market and supports your broader financial journey, leading to greater confidence and success.

5.2 UNDERSTANDING MARKET TRENDS AND INDICATORS

Imagine standing on a beach, observing the waves. Some days, the tide is high, with waves crashing in excitement, and other days, the sea is calm, almost retreating. Similarly, the cryptocurrency market experiences its tides, known as bull and bear markets. In a bull market, asset prices climb, fueled by investor optimism and growing demand, as market participants become increasingly confident in the potential for continued growth. The market is generally buoyant during such periods, with high trading volumes and a pervasive sense of confidence. Investors flock to buy, anticipating further price increases, often driven by positive news, technological advancements, or favorable regulatory changes. In this environment, the key to maximizing gains is identifying the early signs of a bull market and strategically positioning your investments to ride the upward momentum.

On the other hand, a bear market is defined by falling prices, driven by widespread pessimism and fear, as investors grow cautious and risk-averse. In these times, selling pressures build, and many investors choose to exit their positions to minimize losses. The decline is often accompanied by a reduced trading volume, reflecting a lack of interest in buying. This environment can be unsettling but also presents opportunities for those willing to endure the downturn. Understanding bear markets allows you to prepare and capitalize on undervalued assets. Recognizing these shifts in market sentiment is crucial for developing a robust investment strategy, as it informs your decisions on when to buy, hold, or sell.

Market cycles provide a broader perspective on these trends, offering insights into the long-term behavior of the crypto market. These cycles consist of four phases: accumulation, markup, distribution, and markdown. During the accumulation phase, interest in the market is low, and prices are stable, offering a prime opportunity for investors to position themselves for future gains. The markup phase, often called the bull market, is characterized by surging prices and increased investor interest, presenting the best opportunity to realize profits. As the market reaches the distribution phase, prices stabilize, and investors start to sell off their holdings, anticipating a downturn. Finally, the markdown phase—akin to a bear market—sees declining prices, increased fear, and a chance to acquire assets at a discount.

These cycles are not just theoretical; they have been observed in the crypto market, particularly with Bitcoin's historical patterns. Bitcoin's market dominance often sets the tone for the rest of the market, with its halving events acting as catalysts that influence the entire cycle. Understanding these cycles helps investors manage their portfolios more effectively, allowing them to anticipate and adjust to market downturns and capitalize on upswings. By recognizing where the market stands within a cycle, you can tailor your investment decisions to align with prevailing trends, maximizing your potential for growth while minimizing risks.

The interplay of bull and bear markets and the cyclical nature of the crypto market offer a rich landscape for strategic investment. By studying these trends and indicators, you equip yourself with the knowledge to navigate the complexities of the market, making informed decisions that align with your investment goals and risk tolerance. This understanding prepares you for the ups and downs and empowers you to seize opportunities and protect your investments during turbulent times.

5.3 LONG-TERM VS. SHORT-TERM INVESTMENT APPROACHES

Choosing between long-term and short-term strategies can significantly shape your financial outcomes in cryptocurrency investment. Long-term investment, often called "buy and hold," involves purchasing assets to keep them for an extended period, typically years. This approach focuses on building wealth over time, allowing investments to grow with the market's natural ebb and flow. The goal is to capitalize on the overall upward trend of the market, benefiting from compounding growth and the appreciation of assets. In contrast, short-term investment strategies aim to profit from short-lived price movements. These include day trading, swing trading, and scalping, where trades are executed over hours, days, or weeks. The objective is to exploit volatility, capturing gains from the frequent ups and downs in asset prices.

Each strategy has unique benefits and risks. Long-term investing is often associated with stability. It offers the potential for substantial gains, allowing you to ride out market fluctuations without the pressure of constant decision-making. This approach can also mitigate the emotional stress of daily market changes, fostering a sense of patience and discipline. However, long-term investments are not immune to risk; they require a firm conviction in the market's future and the patience to endure downturns.

On the other hand, short-term strategies can yield quick returns and are highly engaging, as they demand active monitoring of market trends. The potential for higher returns is appealing, especially in a volatile market where prices can shift rapidly. Yet, this approach is also fraught with volatility, demanding higher expertise and risk tolerance. The need for constant attention and readiness to react swiftly to market changes can be time-consuming and stressful.

Choosing the right investment approach hinges on aligning your strategy with your financial goals and risk tolerance. Consider your investment style: are you someone who enjoys the thrill of rapid trades and the possibility of immediate gains? Or do you prefer a steadier path, focusing on long-term growth and security? Your strategy should also reflect your life stage. Younger investors might embrace more risk with short-term strategies, seeking to maximize returns early on. In contrast, those nearing retirement may opt for the stability of long-term investments, prioritizing capital preservation and steady growth. It's essential to evaluate how much time and effort you can dedicate to managing your assets and how comfortable you are with potential losses.

Real-world success stories illustrate the effectiveness of both long-term and short-term strategies. Warren Buffett, a renowned long-term investor, exemplifies the power of patience and foresight. His philosophy of value investing—purchasing undervalued assets and holding them for years—has led to substantial wealth accumulation over decades. Buffett's approach underscores the benefits of a consistent, disciplined strategy that withstands market volatility. Conversely, success in short-term trading is exemplified by skilled day traders who thrive in the fast-paced environment of the stock and crypto markets. These traders leverage their expertise in technical analysis and market trends to execute quick trades, often profiting from small price movements. Their success stories highlight the potential for significant returns quickly, driven by a deep understanding of market dynamics and a willingness to embrace risk.

5.4 THE FOUR-YEAR CYCLE: TIMING YOUR INVESTMENTS

Imagine the cryptocurrency market as a grand, cyclical dance, with each step choreographed by a phenomenon known as the four-year cycle. This cycle is a distinct pattern observed in the crypto market, heavily influenced by Bitcoin's halving events. These events occur roughly every four years and involve cutting the reward for mining new Bitcoin blocks in half. This reduction in supply has historically led to significant price increases, as scarcity tends to drive demand. Understanding this cycle is not merely an academic exercise but a strategic tool for predicting market movements, refining investment strategies, and maintaining emotional discipline amidst market volatility.

The cycle's significance becomes evident when examining historical trends. Bitcoin halving events have often preceded dramatic price increases. For instance, following the halving in 2016, Bitcoin's price surged, culminating in the historic bull market of 2017. Similarly, the 2020 halving triggered another wave of exponential growth, propelling Bitcoin and the broader cryptocurrency market to new heights. These patterns are more than coincidences; they reveal the interplay between supply, demand, and investor sentiment. By understanding these dynamics, you can anticipate shifts in market behavior, positioning yourself to make informed and strategic decisions.

The four-year cycle presents distinct phases: accumulation, markup, distribution, and markdown. Each phase offers unique opportunities for investors who can recognize and adapt to the changing landscape. During the accumulation phase, often occurring in bear markets, the mood is dominated by fear and uncertainty. Prices are depressed, and many investors shy away from the market. However, this phase is a golden opportunity for those who understand the cycle's rhythm. You lay the foundation for substantial future gains by accumulating assets at discounted prices.

As the market transitions into the markup phase, optimism begins to return. Prices start climbing, and the market's momentum builds. This phase is characterized by rapid growth, where the value of your portfolio can increase significantly. Identifying the early signs of this transition is key to maximizing your growth potential.

The distribution phase follows, marked by exuberance and widespread participation. Prices reach their peak, and market sentiment is overwhelmingly bullish. While holding on for further gains may be tempting, this phase is the time to realize profits strategically. By selling portions of your holdings, you secure your returns and prepare for the eventual downturn.

Finally, the markdown phase brings declining prices and negative sentiment. This phase is emotionally challenging for many but marks the beginning of a new cycle. The disciplined investor sees this not as a loss but as a fresh opportunity to accumulate undervalued assets and prepare for the next markup phase.

The regularity of the four-year cycle provides a framework for maintaining emotional discipline. By understanding that these phases are a natural part of the market's rhythm, you can detach from short-term noise and focus on long-term objectives.

For instance, during the bear market, when fear is at its peak, and prices are at their lowest, many investors panic and sell their assets. However, recognizing this phase as a recurring opportunity to buy low can help you resist the urge to follow the crowd. Conversely, when prices soar, and euphoria takes over in the bull market, the temptation to hold onto assets indefinitely can be overwhelming. Understanding that the market will eventually cycle back to a downturn enables you to make rational decisions, locking profits at strategic points.

Aligning your investment strategy with the four-year cycle requires a proactive and informed approach. Start by analyzing historical data and familiarizing yourself with the timing of previous halving events. Use this knowledge to anticipate the timing and impact of future cycles. Develop a plan that outlines your actions for each phase, from accumulating assets during bear markets to realizing profits during bull peaks.

Adopting a long-term perspective is the key to navigating the cyclical cryptocurrency market. The cycle's phases may test your patience and emotional resilience. Still, they also offer significant opportunities for those who stay the course. By focusing on overall growth and aligning your strategy with the market's rhythm, you position yourself for sustained success.

Remember, the cryptocurrency market is not a sprint but a marathon. The four-year cycle provides a map, but your discipline, strategic planning and emotional control will guide you to your destination. Embrace the cycle, leverage its regularity, and approach the market with a mindset rooted in patience and purpose. In doing so, you transform the challenges of volatility into opportunities for lasting success.

5.5 ALT SEASON: UNLOCKING OPPORTUNITIES IN THE CRYPTOCURRENCY CYCLE

Alt season is a fascinating and dynamic period in the cryptocurrency market, offering unique opportunities for growth and diversification. It occurs when alternative cryptocurrencies, or altcoins, experience significant price increases and outperform Bitcoin. To fully understand its significance, it is essential to see how alt season integrates into the broader four-year cycle.

Alt season often follows a major Bitcoin rally, typically during the four-year cycle's markup phase. As Bitcoin's price stabilizes after substantial growth, investor attention frequently shifts to altcoins. This shift is driven by the potential for higher percentage gains in altcoins compared to Bitcoin, whose larger market cap often limits its rapid price growth. Several factors contribute to the onset of alt season. Bitcoin's stability is one key trigger. When Bitcoin's price consolidates, investors gain the confidence to explore altcoins.

Additionally, increased market liquidity during bull runs provides the capital needed to drive altcoin growth. Innovative projects and technological advancements within the altcoin space also play a significant role, capturing attention and fueling excitement. Finally, social sentiment, often amplified by online communities and media, creates momentum that drives participation in the altcoin market.

Identifying the early indicators of alt season can help you position yourself to take advantage of its opportunities. One important signal is a decline in Bitcoin dominance, which reflects the growing share of market capitalization held by altcoins. Rising trading volumes in altcoins are another sign, as this indicates increased investor interest and activity. Additionally, specific altcoins often emerge as market leaders, sparking broader interest in the sector. Observing these trends can help you anticipate the start of the alt season.

A disciplined approach is essential to make the most of the alt season. While the possibility of significant returns is unmistakable, the volatility of altcoins also increases risk. Diversification is a critical strategy, as well as spreading your investments across multiple altcoins to mitigate the impact of individual losses. Setting straightforward entry and exit points for each investment is equally important. Defining your goals in advance can avoid emotional decision-making during rapid price fluctuations. When selecting altcoins, prioritize projects with strong fundamentals. Look for coins with active development teams, compelling use cases, and supportive communities. These factors can indicate long-term potential beyond the hype of the alt season. It's also essential to remain vigilant, as alt season can end abruptly. Taking profits strategically ensures you secure gains and avoid being caught off guard by market corrections.

Alt season is not an isolated event but a recurring feature of the cryptocurrency market's natural rhythm. It complements Bitcoin's four-year cycle, adding another opportunity for informed investors. While Bitcoin's halving events and subsequent bull runs drive overall market growth, alt season offers a chance to capitalize on the explosive potential of smaller, innovative projects. Understanding how alt season fits into the cycle provides a strategic advantage. It allows you to see the market as a whole, recognizing the interplay between Bitcoin and altcoins. By aligning your investment strategy with these patterns, you position yourself to navigate the market with confidence and purpose. Alt season represents both excitement and caution. While the opportunity for growth is immense, maintaining discipline and focusing on long-term goals will ensure you maximize the benefits of this dynamic phase in the cryptocurrency market.

5.6 LEVERAGING TECHNOLOGY: APPS AND TOOLS FOR INVESTORS

Imagine standing at the edge of a vast digital landscape, where technology offers a bridge to more intelligent investment decisions. In this realm, investment apps and tools become your allies, providing insights and efficiencies that were once unimaginable. For instance, portfolio trackers are indispensable for real-time monitoring of your investments. They allow you to keep tabs on market trends, track the performance of your assets, and make informed decisions. Tools like CoinStats and CoinTracking give you a comprehensive view of your holdings, ensuring a clear picture of your financial situation. Trading platforms like Binance and Coinbase offer user-friendly interfaces, enabling you to easily buy, sell, and trade cryptocurrencies. These platforms facilitate transactions and provide educational resources, helping you understand the market dynamics better.

The benefits of automation in investing extend far beyond convenience. Automated trading bots, for example, execute trades on your behalf based on pre-set criteria, removing the emotional element that often leads to impulsive decisions. These bots can respond to market changes in seconds, capitalizing on opportunities that human traders might miss. Similarly, rebalancing tools help automatically adjust your portfolio to maintain the target asset allocation, ensuring your investments align with your overall strategy. This automation enhances efficiency, allowing you to focus on broader investment goals rather than daily market fluctuations. By leveraging these technologies, you gain a competitive edge, optimizing your strategy for better returns.

Choosing the right investment tools requires thoughtful evaluation. User reviews and ratings provide valuable feedback on different apps' reliability, functionality, and effectiveness, helping you make more informed decisions. These reviews highlight user experiences, pointing out both strengths and potential drawbacks. Compatibility with your investment strategy is another critical factor. A tool that aligns with your goals and trading style will be more beneficial than one that simply offers the latest features. Consider the specific functions you need—whether it's advanced charting, real-time alerts, or integration with other financial services—and choose tools that cater to those needs. By evaluating these criteria, you ensure that the technology you adopt supports your investment objectives.

Staying technologically adept is not merely an advantage; it's a necessity in modern investing. Keeping up with app updates is crucial, as developers continually enhance features and security measures to improve user experience. Ignoring these updates can leave you with outdated tools, missing out on innovations that could enhance your strategy. Moreover, exploring new technologies and innovations informs you about emerging trends and opportunities. This proactive approach ensures that you remain at the forefront of investment technology, ready to adapt to changes and leverage new tools as they become available. A commitment to technological adaptation can significantly influence your investment success in a fast-evolving digital landscape.

5.7 LEARNING FROM SUCCESSFUL INVESTORS: BEST PRACTICES AND TIPS

Observing the habits of successful investors can provide valuable insights as you enter cryptocurrency investing. One common trait among these investors is discipline. They approach the market with a clear plan, avoiding impulsive decisions driven by short-term market fluctuations. Patience is equally important. It allows them to wait for the right opportunities instead of rushing into trades that may not align with their strategies. These traits enable investors to navigate the volatile crypto landscape, fostering growth steadily.

Continuous learning is another hallmark of successful investors. The cryptocurrency market is dynamic, with new developments emerging regularly. Staying informed about these changes is crucial. Whether it's understanding new technologies, keeping up with regulatory shifts, or analyzing market trends, a commitment to learning equips investors with the knowledge needed to adapt and thrive. This adaptability ensures they remain ahead of the curve, ready to seize opportunities.

Renowned investors offer a wealth of wisdom through their strategies and philosophies. Consider Warren Buffett, who is known for his value investing approach. Buffett advises investing in businesses that demonstrate strong fundamentals and long-term potential. This strategy encourages a focus on intrinsic value rather than short-term market movements. Similarly, Ray Dalio emphasizes diversification to manage risk. By spreading investments across various assets, investors can protect themselves from the volatility of any single asset class. These principles can be applied in the crypto market, guiding you toward a more balanced and informed investment strategy.

While best practices from successful investors offer a solid foundation, it's important to adopt a personalized approach. Tailor strategies to suit your circumstances, considering factors like financial goals, risk tolerance, and available resources. Reflecting on personal investment experiences can provide valuable lessons, inform future decisions, and foster growth. Each investor's path is unique, and adapting strategies to align with personal needs ensures that you remain committed and confident in your investment journey.

5.8 LEARNING FROM FAILURE: LESSONS FROM CRYPTO MISSTEPS

Tales of triumph and failure abound in cryptocurrency, each offering its own lessons. One of the most infamous cases is the collapse of the Mt. Gox exchange. At its peak, Mt. Gox handled approximately 70% of all Bitcoin transactions worldwide. Yet, in 2014, it filed for bankruptcy after losing around 850,000 Bitcoins, a fiasco attributed to security breaches and internal mismanagement. This catastrophic event highlighted the vulnerabilities within the exchange, where inadequate security measures left it susceptible to hacks. The lack of transparency and delayed responses to emerging issues compounded the fallout, leaving many investors without compensation. This incident is a stark reminder of the critical importance of robust security practices and the need for transparency and accountability in financial operations.

Similarly, the rise and subsequent fall of numerous Initial Coin Offerings (ICOs) underscore the potential pitfalls of the crypto space. Many ICOs promised groundbreaking innovations and extraordinary returns, drawing in eager investors. However, many failed to deliver due to poor management and unrealistic expectations. Some projects lacked a viable business model or technical feasibility, while others were outright scams, manipulating investor enthusiasm without intending to launch a legitimate product. These failures have emphasized the necessity for thorough due diligence before investing and the importance of verifying the legitimacy and potential of any crypto project.

From these high-profile failures, we extract valuable lessons to inform future practices. The foremost is the necessity of stringent security measures. Implementing advanced security protocols, such as two-factor authentication and regular security audits, can safeguard against breaches. Exchanges and projects must prioritize transparency, maintaining open communication with stakeholders, and providing timely updates on their operations and challenges. This builds trust and credibility, which is essential for long-term success. Additionally, accountability must be a cornerstone of any crypto venture. Clear governance structures and accountability mechanisms ensure that projects remain focused on their objectives and maintain integrity.

Viewing setbacks as opportunities for growth is vital in the fast-paced world of cryptocurrency. Each failure provides insights that can lead to improved practices and strategies. By cultivating a continuous learning mindset, investors and entrepreneurs can adapt to the evolving landscape, turning past mistakes into stepping stones for future innovation. Embracing resilience allows you to recover from setbacks, reassess strategies, and emerge stronger. Community support and collaboration play a crucial role in this process. Engaging with peers, sharing experiences, and learning from others can provide valuable perspectives and encouragement during challenging times.

As we reflect on these lessons, it's clear that the path to success in cryptocurrency is not without its hurdles. By acknowledging and learning from failures, we can forge a more resilient and informed approach that is better equipped to navigate the complexities of the crypto market. The experiences of the past illuminate the way forward, guiding us in building a more secure and transparent crypto environment. This chapter highlights the importance of learning from failure, setting the stage for our upcoming exploration of safeguarding investments. As we move forward, we'll explore strategies to protect your assets, ensuring your investment endeavors are prosperous and secure.

CHAPTER 6
EXPLORING THE POTENTIAL OF BLOCKCHAIN TECHNOLOGY

Imagine a vast library where every book is tracked and recorded in real-time. You can see who borrowed a book, when it was checked out, and where it currently resides. Blockchain technology offers this level of transparency and traceability to the supply chain management world. Verifying product authenticity and origin is vital in the intricate global supply chain. Blockchain provides a tamper-evident ledger that enhances transparency among participants. Each transaction, whether the movement of goods or the transfer of ownership, is recorded and accessible to all parties involved. This shared visibility builds trust and reduces sourcing, transport, and distribution risks. Companies like Mitsubishi and De Beers have embraced blockchain to trace product origins, ensuring ethical sourcing and compliance with environmental, social, and governance (ESG) standards. Blockchain offers a robust solution for modern supply chain challenges by reducing administrative costs and enhancing data reliability.

6.1 TRANSFORMING INDUSTRIES WITH BLOCKCHAIN TECHNOLOGY

The healthcare sector encounters distinct challenges, especially regarding data security and patient privacy. Blockchain technology promises to revolutionize healthcare by providing secure and efficient medical records management. Blockchain enables the secure transfer of patient data between healthcare providers, guaranteeing that sensitive information remains private and immune to tampering. This secure sharing enhances collaboration between medical professionals, leading to better patient outcomes. Moreover, blockchain's immutable nature helps prevent fraud in medical billing. Maintaining a transparent and unchangeable record of transactions makes it difficult for fraudulent activities to go unnoticed. For instance, patient consent management, a critical aspect of clinical trials, can benefit from blockchain's ability to ensure that consent records are stored transparently, providing accountability and traceability.

In democratic processes, blockchain technology offers a new way to conduct secure and transparent elections. Traditional voting systems face challenges such as tampering and voter fraud. Blockchain introduces a solution by creating tamper-proof voting records that multiple parties can verify. Every vote is captured on the blockchain, ensuring that any attempt to alter it is immediately detectable. This transparency builds trust in the electoral process, as voters can verify their votes are counted accurately.

Additionally, blockchain improves voter identity verification, minimizing the risk of fraudulent voting. By ensuring that only eligible voters can cast their ballots, blockchain technology strengthens the integrity of elections. This innovation boosts voter confidence and encourages higher participation, fostering more equitable democratic processes.

Intellectual property protection is another area where blockchain's capabilities shine. Creators often struggle to protect their rights in the digital age, where unauthorized use and distribution of content are rampant. Blockchain offers a solution through digital rights management, allowing creators to register their works on a public ledger. This registration provides a verifiable record of ownership, making it easier to assert rights and pursue legal action if necessary. Furthermore, blockchain enables tracking the usage of creative works, ensuring that creators receive due credit and compensation. This transparency fosters a fairer environment for artists, musicians, and writers, empowering them to control how their creations are used and monetized. As blockchain continues to evolve, its applications in intellectual property protection will likely expand, offering new opportunities for creativity and innovation.

Reflection Exercise: Real-World Blockchain Applications

Consider how blockchain technology might impact an industry you're interested in. Reflect on the potential benefits and challenges of implementing blockchain solutions. How could transparency, security, or traceability improve current practices? Write down your thoughts and explore how these innovations could reshape traditional systems.

These examples illustrate how blockchain extends beyond cryptocurrency, offering transformative solutions across various sectors. Its capacity to enhance transparency, security, and trust makes it a powerful tool for addressing complex challenges. As you explore these applications, consider how blockchain might influence industries you're passionate about and envision the possibilities it brings to the future.

6.2 SMART CONTRACTS: AUTOMATING AGREEMENTS

Imagine a world where contracts execute automatically, eliminating the need for intermediaries. This is the promise of smart contracts, a transformative feature of blockchain technology. These digital agreements are encoded in computer protocols that automatically enforce and verify the terms of a contract. Unlike traditional contracts, which rely on trust between parties or an intermediary to oversee the agreement, smart contracts operate independently. They are designed to execute specific actions when predetermined conditions are met, eliminating the need for third-party involvement. This simplifies processes and reduces the likelihood of errors or disputes, as the terms are immutable and transparent on the blockchain. The impact of this technology extends far beyond mere efficiency, influencing cost, security, and trust in once unimaginable ways.

There are numerous benefits to smart contracts compared to traditional contracts. Firstly, they offer increased efficiency, as the automation of processes significantly reduces the time required to execute agreements. Imagine the tedious back-and-forth emails, phone calls, and meetings often necessary to finalize a deal. Smart contracts are rendered obsolete, as the contract itself handles execution. Secondly, by removing intermediaries, smart contracts help reduce costs. Parties can save significant amounts of money without the need to pay for services like legal oversight or escrow. This cost-effectiveness is especially valuable for small businesses and startups with limited resources. Furthermore, smart contracts enhance security; the decentralized nature of blockchain ensures that once a contract is created, it cannot be altered without consensus from the network. This immutability protects the agreement's integrity, reducing the risk of fraud or manipulation.

Smart contracts find application across various industries, each showcasing their versatility and transformative potential. In the insurance sector, they can automate payouts. For example, in the case of a flight delay, a smart contract could automatically initiate a compensation payment to affected passengers once verified data sources confirm the delay. This removes the need for claims to be filed and processed manually, creating a smoother experience for policyholders. In real estate, smart contracts can revolutionize property transactions. When the terms of a sale are met, such as the transfer of funds, the smart contract could automatically transfer ownership to the buyer. This speeds up the process and reduces the potential for disputes, as all conditions are pre-agreed and encoded into the contract. These examples illustrate how smart contracts can bring greater transparency and efficiency to traditional industries, altering how agreements are made and executed.

Despite their promising potential, smart contracts are not without challenges. One significant hurdle is their code-based nature, which introduces vulnerabilities. If a smart contract contains programming errors or security vulnerabilities, malicious actors could exploit them, resulting in financial losses. The infamous DAO attack on Ethereum in 2016 serves as a cautionary tale, where vulnerabilities in smart contract code resulted in a substantial loss of funds. Addressing these vulnerabilities requires rigorous testing, audits, coding standards, and practice improvements. Another challenge is legal recognition. As smart contracts are an emerging technology, current legal frameworks may not fully acknowledge or support their use. This can create uncertainties around enforcement and liability, especially in jurisdictions where digital signatures or electronic contracts are not legally binding. Overcoming these challenges will require collaboration between technologists, legal experts, and policymakers to create robust frameworks that ensure smart contracts' safe and effective use.

Smart contracts hold the potential to radically alter the way agreements are made and executed, offering speed, cost savings, and security. Their use across diverse applications, from insurance to real estate, illustrates their versatility and impact. However, addressing their vulnerabilities and legal recognition will be crucial for broader adoption. As the technology matures, smart contracts may become a cornerstone of our digital economy, seamlessly integrating into everyday transactions and transforming industries.

6.3 DECENTRALIZED FINANCE (DEFI): THE NEXT FRONTIER

In the changing world of finance, decentralized finance, or DeFi, signifies a major shift that disrupts traditional financial systems. Unlike conventional banking, which relies heavily on centralized institutions to facilitate transactions and manage financial services, DeFi utilizes blockchain technology to establish a decentralized network where individuals can conduct financial transactions directly with each other. This peer-to-peer model removes the need for intermediaries, fundamentally transforming the delivery of financial services. For example, peer-to-peer lending platforms within DeFi allow people to lend and borrow funds from one another, setting their own terms and interest rates. This democratizes access to credit and offers potentially higher returns for lenders than traditional savings accounts. Similarly, decentralized exchanges (DEXs) operate without a central authority, enabling users to trade cryptocurrencies directly in a secure, transparent environment. By removing central intermediaries, DeFi increases the efficiency of financial transactions while maintaining user autonomy.

The benefits of DeFi are considerable, making it an attractive option for those previously excluded from the financial system. A major advantage is improved accessibility. DeFi platforms are accessible to anyone with an internet connection, removing the geographical and socio-economic barriers that traditionally restrict access to financial services. This inclusivity allows individuals in underbanked regions to participate in the global economy. Additionally, DeFi platforms often feature lower transaction fees than those traditional financial institutions charge. DeFi reduces overhead costs by cutting out intermediaries, allowing users to receive more value from their transactions. This cost-effectiveness particularly appeals to small investors and startups seeking efficient, affordable financial solutions. The transparency built into blockchain technology also promotes trust among users, as all transactions are logged on a public ledger, making verification straightforward and reducing the potential for fraud.

Several popular applications illustrate the diverse possibilities within the DeFi space. Uniswap, a leading decentralized exchange, enables users to trade tokens without relying on a centralized platform, boosting liquidity and simplifying access. The platform exemplifies the decentralized ethos by using smart contracts to automate transactions, executing trades based on predefined criteria. Another notable platform is Aave, a decentralized lending service that lets users lend or borrow cryptocurrencies. Aave's flash loans are one of its key innovations, allowing users to borrow funds without collateral, provided the loan is repaid within the same transaction block. These applications showcase the versatility and innovation driving the DeFi movement, providing users with novel ways to manage their assets and engage with the financial system.

However, the fast-changing DeFi landscape comes with its own set of challenges and risks. A significant concern is the security of smart contracts, which are the backbone of DeFi operations. While smart contracts automate processes and reduce human error, they are also susceptible to programming flaws and vulnerabilities. Malicious actors can exploit these weaknesses, resulting in significant financial losses for users. The infamous DAO hack is a stark reminder of the potential dangers of poorly coded contracts.

Additionally, the regulatory environment surrounding DeFi remains uncertain as governments and regulatory bodies struggle to determine how to classify and regulate these decentralized platforms. This lack of clarity can pose legal risks for users and developers alike, potentially hindering the growth and adoption of DeFi solutions. As DeFi matures, addressing these security and regulatory challenges will ensure its sustainability and success.

Decentralized finance represents a bold reimagining of financial services, offering increased accessibility, efficiency, and innovation. By empowering individuals to interact directly with one another, DeFi challenges traditional models and opens new possibilities for financial inclusion and autonomy. Yet, as with any emerging technology, it carries inherent risks that must be carefully managed. Understanding these dynamics is essential for anyone considering participation in the DeFi ecosystem.

6.4 NFTS: THE INTERSECTION OF ART AND TECHNOLOGY

Non-fungible tokens, or NFTs, have emerged as a novel form of digital asset, distinct from their fungible counterparts like cryptocurrencies. Unlike Bitcoin or Ethereum, which are interchangeable and hold the same value as one another, each NFT is unique and cannot be exchanged on a one-to-one basis for another NFT. This indivisibility is a defining characteristic, making NFTs suitable for representing ownership of rare digital items. Each token is embedded with metadata that verifies its authenticity and ownership and is recorded on the blockchain. This ensures that the provenance of the digital asset is transparent and unalterable, offering a level of trust that is hard to attain with traditional digital files.

The art world has undergone a seismic shift with the rise of NFTs, fundamentally transforming how art is created, bought, and sold. Digital art, once easily replicable and challenging to monetize, now finds a new avenue for valuation and exchange. Artists can mint their works as NFTs, thus ensuring that each piece is a one-of-a-kind digital item with verifiable ownership. This process has opened up new revenue streams for artists, who can now sell digital artwork directly to collectors without intermediaries. Furthermore, NFTs allow automatic royalties to be programmed. This means that whenever an NFT is resold, a percentage of the sale is returned to the original artist, ensuring they continue to benefit from their work over time. Such arrangements were challenging in the traditional art market, where artists often lost control of their work once sold.

Beyond the art world, NFTs have begun to carve a niche in the entertainment and media sectors, offering innovative ways for creators to engage with their audiences. In the music industry, artists use NFTs to release exclusive tracks or albums, providing fans with unique memorabilia and access to content. This model allows musicians to forge closer connections with their audience, bypassing traditional distribution channels. Similarly, in the film industry, NFTs are being used to sell digital collectibles, such as behind-the-scenes footage or concept art, to dedicated fans. Virtual real estate is another burgeoning area where NFTs represent ownership of digital land in virtual worlds. These properties can be bought, sold, and developed, creating a parallel economy where users can invest and interact in entirely digital spaces.

Despite their growing popularity, NFTs face controversies and criticisms that challenge their sustainability and appeal. One of the primary concerns is their environmental impact. The creation and transaction of NFTs often involve energy-intensive processes, mainly due to the blockchain networks on which they reside. These networks, particularly those using proof-of-work consensus mechanisms, consume significant electricity, leading to a substantial carbon footprint. This issue has sparked debate about the environmental responsibility of digital artists and collectors, prompting some to explore more eco-friendly blockchain alternatives.

Additionally, the NFT market is known for its volatility, with the value of tokens subject to rapid fluctuations. This instability can deter potential investors, as market trends are difficult to predict, leading to significant financial risk. For artists and creators, navigating this volatile landscape requires careful consideration of market dynamics and potential long-term value.

NFTs represent a fascinating convergence of art and technology, offering unprecedented opportunities for creators and collectors alike. Their ability to authenticate digital ownership has already begun reshaping the art world and extending into music, film, and virtual real estate. However, their challenges, from environmental concerns to market volatility, highlight the need for ongoing innovation and adaptation. As the NFT space continues to evolve, it will be crucial for participants to strike a balance between embracing new possibilities and addressing the pressing issues that accompany this digital revolution.

6.5 BLOCKCHAIN IN DIFFERENT INDUSTRIES: REAL-WORLD EXAMPLES

In logistics, blockchain technology is reshaping how goods are tracked and documented, offering unprecedented transparency and efficiency. IBM's Food Trust network is a prime example of this transformation. By leveraging blockchain, this network allows participants to trace the journey of food products from farm to table with remarkable precision. Each transaction, from harvesting to shipping to retail, is logged on an immutable ledger, reducing the time needed to track a product's origin from days to seconds. This transparency not only enhances consumer confidence but also allows for quicker responses in the event of a food safety issue, minimizing the impact of recalls and ensuring that only affected products are removed from shelves.

Similarly, Maersk's TradeLens platform has revolutionized the shipping industry by creating a digital ecosystem connecting various supply chain stakeholders. Through blockchain, TradeLens streamlines documentation processes, reducing the reliance on paper-based systems that are often slow and prone to errors. This digitalization enables real-time visibility into shipment data, allowing for better coordination and decision-making among suppliers, shippers, and regulators. By fostering greater collaboration and trust, TradeLens helps reduce shipping times and costs while improving overall supply chain efficiency. These case studies illustrate blockchain's potential to address long-standing logistics challenges, paving the way for a more transparent and efficient global trade network.

In the energy sector, blockchain facilitates the transition towards decentralized energy grids, empowering consumers to participate actively in energy markets. By enabling peer-to-peer energy trading, blockchain allows individuals to directly buy and sell excess energy generated from renewable sources, such as solar panels, with their neighbors. This decentralization encourages the adoption of clean energy and reduces reliance on traditional utility companies. By recording transactions on a blockchain, participants can ensure their trades are secure and transparent, fostering trust in the system. This innovative approach to energy management has the potential to revolutionize the way we consume and distribute power, making energy systems more resilient and sustainable.

Blockchain is making significant strides in education, particularly in verifying academic credentials. With the proliferation of digital diplomas, students and employers face challenges in ensuring the authenticity of educational qualifications. Blockchain offers a solution by providing a secure platform for storing and verifying academic records. Institutions can issue digital diplomas recorded on a blockchain, allowing graduates to share their credentials with potential employers easily. This eliminates the need for traditional paper-based transcripts, which can be cumbersome to verify and susceptible to forgery. Additionally, blockchain's secure certificate storage ensures that academic records remain accurate and accessible throughout a student's lifetime, simplifying the credential verification process for individuals and institutions.

Government services also benefit from integrating blockchain technology, particularly in public administration. Land registry systems, for instance, have long been plagued by inefficiencies and corruption, making property transactions cumbersome and prone to disputes. By implementing blockchain, governments can create a transparent and tamper-proof record of land ownership, reducing the risk of fraud and streamlining the buying and selling process. This enhances trust in property transactions and reduces the time and cost of registering land. Moreover, blockchain plays a crucial role in digital identity management, enabling citizens to securely store and manage their personal information. By providing a decentralized platform for identity verification, blockchain can simplify interactions with government services, reducing the need for multiple forms of identification and making it easier for individuals to access the services they need. These applications demonstrate blockchain's transformative potential in improving government operations' efficiency and transparency, offering new ways to enhance public trust and engagement.

6.6 ANTICIPATING FUTURE TRENDS: WHERE IS BLOCKCHAIN HEADED?

As we stand on the brink of a technological revolution, the evolution of blockchain technology continues to capture imaginations and drive innovation. One of the most promising areas of development is scalability. Current blockchain networks often struggle with transaction speed and capacity, which limits their ability to efficiently handle large volumes of data. To address this, developers are working on enhanced scalability solutions, such as sharding and layer-two protocols. These advancements aim to increase throughput, allowing blockchain to support more transactions per second without compromising security. As these solutions mature, blockchain will become more viable for widespread use across various sectors.

Integrating blockchain with the Internet of Things (IoT) presents another exciting frontier. IoT devices generate vast amounts of data, requiring secure and efficient ways to manage and share this information. Blockchain offers a decentralized and transparent method for recording IoT data, ensuring it remains tamper-proof and accessible to authorized parties. This integration can revolutionize healthcare and agriculture industries, where real-time data tracking and analysis can improve outcomes. As IoT devices become more prevalent, their collaboration with blockchain technology will likely enhance the functionality and reliability of both systems.

Cross-industry collaboration is another area where blockchain's potential shines. By providing a shared digital infrastructure, blockchain enables different industries to work together seamlessly. For example, a supply chain network might integrate with a financial institution's blockchain to streamline payment processes and improve transparency. This shared infrastructure reduces the need for multiple systems, fostering efficiency and lowering costs. Furthermore, it encourages innovation by allowing organizations to leverage each other's strengths and expertise, creating new opportunities for growth and development. As businesses recognize these benefits, we expect more partnerships to form across sectors, further driving blockchain adoption.

Regulatory developments will play a critical role in shaping the future of blockchain. Efforts toward global standardization are underway to create a cohesive framework that ensures compliance and security across jurisdictions. Such standardization will facilitate cross-border transactions and enhance trust in blockchain systems. Regulatory clarity is essential for businesses and investors, providing a stable environment for innovation and growth. However, achieving this global consensus will require cooperation and dialogue among governments, industry leaders, and regulatory bodies. As these discussions progress, they will influence how blockchain technology is implemented and regulated worldwide.

Emerging technologies like artificial intelligence (AI) and quantum computing complement blockchain by providing additional layers of innovation and security. AI can analyze vast amounts of data generated by blockchain networks, identifying patterns and optimizing processes. This synergy enhances decision-making and allows for more efficient resource allocation. On the other hand, with its unparalleled processing power, quantum computing offers the potential to solve complex cryptographic challenges that could threaten blockchain security. By integrating these technologies, blockchain can evolve to meet future demands, ensuring its continued relevance and resilience.

The societal impact of widespread blockchain adoption could be profound. Decentralized governance models, enabled by blockchain, offer an alternative to traditional hierarchical systems. These models promote transparency and accountability by distributing decision-making power among stakeholders, potentially transforming organizations' and governments' operations. Enhanced data privacy is another potential benefit. Blockchain's ability to provide secure and transparent data management can empower individuals to control their personal information, reducing the risk of data breaches and misuse. This shift towards greater privacy and autonomy can redefine relationships between individuals, businesses, and governments, fostering a more equitable digital landscape.

As we explore these potential developments, it's clear that blockchain holds the promise of reshaping numerous aspects of our world. From scalability improvements to cross-industry collaborations, the future of blockchain is bright. Regulatory frameworks and emerging technologies will guide its evolution, ensuring it meets the needs of an increasingly interconnected society. Blockchain's potential to enhance governance and privacy offers exciting possibilities for the future, making this technology a cornerstone of the digital age.

CHAPTER 7
ADDRESSING COMMON CONCERNS AND MISUNDERSTANDINGS

Imagine you're about to embark on a digital adventure, navigating cryptocurrency's exciting yet intricate terrain. You're armed with curiosity and ambition, ready to explore the possibilities. But as you venture more profoundly, you encounter tales of hacking incidents and exchange failures that seem like ominous clouds over your journey. These stories are not just myths; they reflect real vulnerabilities within cryptocurrency systems that can impact your investments. Hacking incidents, for instance, are a significant threat. Cybercriminals target exchanges and digital wallets to steal funds, exploiting weaknesses in security measures. Exchange failures, another concern, can occur when platforms collapse due to poor management or security breaches, leaving users unable to access their funds. These risks highlight the importance of being vigilant and informed about the potential dangers in the crypto space.

7.1 ESSENTIAL SECURITY MEASURES FOR PROTECTING YOUR DIGITAL ASSETS

To protect your digital assets, implementing robust security strategies is crucial. Utilizing cold storage solutions is one effective way to safeguard your cryptocurrencies. Cold storage involves keeping your digital coins offline and away from internet threats, thus reducing the risk of hacking. Hardware wallets, like Ledger and Trezor, are popular cold storage options. They store your private keys securely offline, ensuring your assets remain safe even if your computer is compromised. Regular software updates are another essential practice. Developers continuously work to patch vulnerabilities and enhance security features, so keeping your devices and wallets up to date is imperative. Implementing two-factor authentication (2FA) provides an additional layer of protection. This security measure requires a second verification form, such as a code sent to your phone, making unauthorized access much more difficult.

The landscape of crypto security is continuously evolving, with new technologies emerging to protect digital assets further. Multi-signature wallets are one such innovation, offering enhanced security by requiring multiple signatures from different devices or parties to authorize a transaction. This means that even if one of your devices is compromised, a hacker still needs access to the others to complete a transaction. Hardware security modules (HSMs) are another advancement, providing a physical device that manages digital keys and performs cryptographic operations. These modules are designed to be tamper-proof, ensuring your keys remain secure even if the device is physically attacked. By adopting these cutting-edge technologies, you can significantly enhance the security of your cryptocurrency holdings.

Despite these advancements, misconceptions about cryptocurrency safety persist. One common misunderstanding is that blockchain technology itself is inherently insecure. In reality, blockchain is designed to be secure by nature, with its decentralized structure and cryptographic processes providing robust protection against tampering. However, it is essential to recognize that while the blockchain may be secure, its platforms and applications can still be vulnerable if not adequately protected. Another myth is the notion of impenetrable privacy. While cryptocurrencies can offer a degree of anonymity, they are not entirely private. Transactions are recorded on a public ledger, which can be traced and analyzed. This transparency is a double-edged sword, offering security and accountability and requiring users to be mindful of their privacy practices.

To reinforce your understanding, consider using a checklist to evaluate your current security measures and identify areas for improvement. This exercise will help you ensure that you take the necessary steps to protect your digital assets. Regularly review your security practices, stay informed about the latest developments in crypto security, and remain vigilant against emerging threats. Doing so lets you confidently navigate cryptocurrency, knowing your investments are well-protected.

Security Measures Checklist

- Utilize cold storage solutions for long-term holdings.
- Regularly update software and applications.
- Implement two-factor authentication on all accounts.
- Consider multi-signature wallets for enhanced security.
- Safeguard private keys and avoid storing them online.
- Stay informed about the latest security technologies and practices.

7.2 CRYPTOCURRENCY AND ENVIRONMENTAL IMPACT: THE TRUTH

As you explore the world of cryptocurrency, it's essential to understand the environmental concerns that come with it. Crypto mining relies heavily on proof-of-work systems, especially for coins like Bitcoin. These systems require immense computational power, consuming vast amounts of energy. Mining farms, often located in countries with lower electricity costs, contribute significantly to this demand. The carbon footprint from these operations is substantial, with emissions comparable to those of entire countries. This environmental impact has sparked debates about the sustainability of cryptocurrencies and the ethical implications of their energy consumption. However, it's not just about the energy used; it's also about how it's generated. Many mining operations depend on fossil fuels, adding to their carbon footprint. This reliance on non-renewable energy sources raises questions about the long-term viability of such practices.

Efforts to mitigate the environmental impact of crypto mining are gaining momentum. Some companies and initiatives are exploring the transition to renewable energy sources. Mining operations can significantly reduce carbon emissions by harnessing solar, wind, or hydroelectric power. This shift lessens environmental harm and aligns with global sustainability goals. Developing energy-efficient mining hardware also plays a crucial role in minimizing resource consumption. Newer, more advanced technologies are being designed to perform the same computational tasks using less energy. These advancements signal a growing awareness within the industry of the need to balance innovation with environmental responsibility. As these efforts evolve, they offer hope for a more sustainable future for crypto mining.

An alternative path towards more eco-friendly cryptocurrency operations lies in adopting different consensus mechanisms. Proof of stake is one such mechanism that offers a less energy-intensive solution. Unlike proof of work, which requires miners to solve complex equations, proof of stake selects validators based on the number of coins they hold and are willing to "stake" as collateral. This method reduces the need for excessive computational power, thereby lowering energy consumption. Delegated proof of stake takes this concept further by allowing coin holders to elect delegates who validate transactions on their behalf. This approach enhances efficiency and reduces the environmental impact even more. These mechanisms provide greener alternatives and open the door to faster and more scalable blockchain technologies.

To fully grasp the environmental impact of cryptocurrencies, it's helpful to compare them to traditional financial systems. While the energy consumption of crypto mining is often highlighted, the banking infrastructure also demands substantial energy. Banks operate a vast network that consumes significant resources, from data centers to ATMs. In some cases, the energy use of the traditional banking system can rival that of cryptocurrencies. However, blockchain technologies offer unique opportunities for environmental conservation. For instance, they can improve supply chain transparency and efficiency, reducing waste and better resource management. By providing a secure and immutable record of transactions, blockchain can support eco-friendly practices across various industries. This potential for positive impact underscores the importance of viewing cryptocurrencies as energy consumers and tools for broader environmental progress.

7.3 OVERCOMING THE FEAR OF MISSING OUT (FOMO)

Navigating the cryptocurrency landscape can often feel overwhelming, especially when faced with the phenomenon known as FOMO or the Fear of Missing Out. This psychological response frequently influences decision-making in the crypto market, driven by the emotional triggers of excitement and urgency. Investors often see others reaping profits and fear they might miss their opportunity. This emotional whirlwind can lead to impulsive buying and selling, where decisions are made not on analysis but on the anxiety of being left behind. Such behavior can distort rational thinking and cause individuals to chase trends without due diligence, leading to unfavorable outcomes. The crypto market is particularly susceptible to this because of its volatility and the speed at which information spreads. The constant barrage of news and social media updates can amplify these emotions, creating a feedback loop of anxiety and impulsivity.

To effectively manage FOMO, adopting strategies anchoring your decision-making process is crucial. One practical approach is setting predetermined investment criteria. By establishing clear guidelines for when to buy or sell, you create a framework that helps resist emotional impulses. This disciplined approach ensures that your actions are based on logic and analysis rather than fleeting emotions. By staying present and aware of your feelings, you can better recognize when FOMO influences your decisions. Mindfulness allows you to pause, reflect, and make choices that align with your long-term goals rather than immediate reactions. This conscious awareness helps calm the mind, reduce the sway of emotions, and empower you to make informed decisions. These strategies, coupled with regular reflection on your investment goals, can significantly mitigate the impact of FOMO and enhance your overall trading experience.

Long-term thinking is a vital component in combating FOMO's influence. Focusing on broader investment goals shifts your attention from short-term market fluctuations to the bigger picture. Developing a disciplined investment plan that prioritizes your financial objectives over immediate gains can provide stability and clarity. This plan should include a diversified portfolio that spreads risk across different assets, reducing the pressure to act on short-term trends. By setting realistic targets and timelines, you create a roadmap that guides your investment journey, helping you stay committed to your strategy even when the market is volatile. Long-term thinking enhances your ability to withstand market fluctuations and fosters a sense of patience and resilience, essential qualities for navigating the crypto landscape. This approach encourages you to view your investments as part of a broader financial strategy, aligning your actions with your long-term vision.

Consider the case of a market bubble, a scenario where FOMO-driven mistakes are particularly evident. During a bubble, asset prices inflate rapidly as investors rush to buy, driven by the fear of missing out on profits. The dot-com bubble of the late 1990s is a classic example, where tech stocks soared to unsustainable levels before crashing. In the cryptocurrency world, a similar situation occurred with the 2017 Bitcoin surge. As prices skyrocketed, many investors bought in without fully understanding the market dynamics or potential risks. When the bubble burst, those who acted on FOMO faced significant losses. These real-world scenarios illustrate the dangers of allowing FOMO to dictate investment decisions. They serve as cautionary tales, reminding us of the importance of maintaining a disciplined approach and focusing on long-term goals. By learning from these examples, you can better navigate the complexities of the crypto market and avoid the pitfalls of impulsive decision-making.

As you move forward, remember that managing FOMO is an ongoing process. It requires vigilance, self-awareness, and a commitment to staying informed and grounded in your investment strategy. By cultivating these qualities, you empower yourself to make decisions that align with your financial goals, ensuring a more stable and rewarding experience in cryptocurrency.

7.4 THE ROLE OF COMMUNITY: FINDING SUPPORT AND RESOURCES

Engaging with a supportive crypto community can profoundly enhance your experience in the cryptocurrency world. The power of a community lies in its ability to bring together individuals with shared interests and goals. Participating in these groups gives you access to knowledge and insights that can accelerate your learning and understanding. Members often share their experiences, discuss market trends, and provide advice based on their successes and failures. This collective wisdom can be invaluable, offering perspectives you might not have considered. Moreover, the community provides moral support, especially in a field as volatile and unpredictable as cryptocurrency. It's reassuring to know you're not navigating this complex landscape alone and that others have faced and overcome the same challenges. This sense of belonging can bolster your confidence and encourage you to persevere, even when the market seems daunting.

Connecting with like-minded individuals is easier than ever, thanks to the plethora of online platforms dedicated to cryptocurrency discussions. Online forums and social media groups serve as vibrant hubs to engage with others, ask questions, and share your thoughts. Platforms like Reddit's r/CryptoCurrency offer extensive threads where users discuss everything from market analysis to technical developments. These forums are a treasure trove of information, allowing you to learn from experts and fellow beginners. Social media groups, particularly Discord and Telegram, provide real-time interaction and foster a sense of immediacy and connection. These channels often host live discussions, Q&A sessions, and even virtual meetups, allowing you to interact with others in a dynamic setting. Beyond the digital realm, attending meetups and conferences can further deepen your engagement. These events offer networking opportunities, learning from industry leaders, and participating in workshops that enhance your skills. By immersing yourself in these communities, you build relationships supporting your journey through the ever-evolving crypto landscape.

Community-driven projects highlight the innovative spirit that thrives when individuals collaborate. Open-source development is a prime example, where developers worldwide contribute to projects, driving innovation and growth. These collaborative efforts result in robust, adaptable software that benefits from diverse perspectives and expertise. By participating in or supporting open-source projects, you become part of a more significant movement that pushes the boundaries of what's possible with blockchain technology. Crowdsourced problem-solving is another avenue where community involvement shines. Complex challenges can be addressed through collective brainstorming, with solutions emerging from the combined efforts of individuals across the globe. This collaborative approach leads to innovative outcomes and fosters a sense of camaraderie and shared purpose. The impact of these projects extends beyond the technical realm, influencing policy, education, and community engagement, demonstrating the power of collective action in shaping the future of cryptocurrency.

Several influential crypto communities have emerged as leaders in fostering engagement and collaboration. Reddit's r/CryptoCurrency, with its vast user base, stands as a cornerstone for discussion and information sharing. It offers a platform for debates, insights, and the latest news, making it a go-to resource for anyone interested in crypto. Discord and Telegram channels, on the other hand, provide more focused and interactive environments. These channels often cater to specific projects, technologies, or trading strategies, allowing you to dive deeper into areas of interest. They facilitate direct communication with project developers, influencers, and other enthusiasts, creating an atmosphere of real-time learning and collaboration. These communities are about information exchange, building networks, finding mentors, and growing together. Engaging with these platforms offers opportunities to expand your knowledge, gain new insights, and make connections that can significantly impact your cryptocurrency experience.

7.5 CRITICALLY EVALUATING CRYPTOCURRENCY NEWS AND TRENDS

In the rapidly evolving world of cryptocurrency, news and trends are pivotal in shaping perceptions and influencing decisions. Yet, not all information is created equal. The necessity for critical thinking when consuming crypto news cannot be overstated. Amidst the flood of headlines, distinguishing between fact and opinion is a skill that can protect you from making misguided decisions. Sensationalism often dominates the narrative, with exaggerated claims or unverified reports leading to skewed perceptions. Being skeptical helps you see beyond the hype and assess the substance of what's being presented. This discernment is crucial in a field where misinformation can lead to costly mistakes. By questioning the validity of what you read, you build a foundation for informed decision-making, empowering yourself to navigate the crypto landscape more confidently.

When assessing the credibility of news sources, several strategies can help ensure the information you rely on is trustworthy. One key approach is to check the credentials of the author or publication. Reputable sources often have a history of accurate reporting and a team of experts. Look for authors with a track record in the crypto industry or related fields. Cross-referencing multiple sources is another valuable technique. By comparing reports from different outlets, you can identify consistencies and discrepancies, which can indicate the reliability of the information. This practice enhances your understanding and protects you from biased or misleading narratives. In a landscape where rumors can spread rapidly, verifying facts with multiple sources is a safeguard against misinformation, helping you build a more precise and accurate picture of the crypto environment.

Bias and misinformation are common pitfalls in crypto reporting, often distorting reality and influencing investor behavior. Overhyping new developments is frequent, where minor advancements are portrayed as revolutionary breakthroughs. Such exaggerations can create unrealistic expectations, leading to market volatility when the reality fails to meet the hype. Ignoring counterarguments is another form of bias that can skew your perception. Balanced reporting considers different perspectives, offering a more comprehensive view of the situation. By being aware of these biases, you can approach the news with a critical eye, questioning the motives behind the reports and seeking a more nuanced understanding. This awareness ensures that your decisions are based on a well-rounded perspective rather than being swayed by singular narratives that may not reflect the truth.

Proactive information gathering is essential to stay informed and critically engaged with ongoing trends. Setting up news alerts for specific topics or keywords allows you to receive timely updates without being inundated with unnecessary information. This targeted approach ensures you stay informed about developments relevant to your interests. Following diverse perspectives and experts in the field can also enrich your understanding. Engaging with various voices gives you insights into different aspects of the crypto world, from technological innovations to regulatory changes. This diversity of thought encourages critical analysis and helps you form a more balanced view of the market. Engaging with thought leaders and experts through social media, blogs, and podcasts can provide valuable context and depth, enhancing your ability to evaluate news and trends critically.

As you cultivate these skills, you'll find yourself better equipped to navigate the complexities of cryptocurrency news and trends. Your ability to discern fact from fiction, recognize bias, and seek diverse viewpoints will empower you to make informed decisions grounded in a comprehensive understanding of the ever-changing crypto landscape. This chapter has explored the importance of critical thinking, but the journey doesn't end here. As you continue exploring, remember that knowledge is your greatest ally in cryptocurrency, guiding you through the challenges and opportunities.

7.6 UNDERSTANDING BLACK SWAN EVENTS IN CRYPTOCURRENCY

Black swan events refer to infrequent and unforeseen incidents that can have significant and widespread effects on global systems, including the cryptocurrency market. Understanding these events and their potential effects is crucial for navigating the volatile world of digital assets. Just as choosing a secure exchange is essential for safeguarding your investments, preparing for black swan events involves a proactive approach to risk management and adaptability.

A black swan event could manifest as a major regulatory crackdown, a sudden technological failure, or an unforeseen geopolitical conflict that disrupts the broader financial ecosystem. These events often lead to sharp market fluctuations, challenging even the most seasoned traders. For example, in 2020, the global COVID-19 pandemic triggered a black swan event that disrupted financial markets worldwide. In cryptocurrency, Bitcoin initially saw a sharp drop in value as investors panicked but later rebounded significantly as interest in decentralized and digital assets surged amid economic uncertainty. Similarly, a significant hack or security breach in a leading exchange can erode trust and cause widespread panic in the cryptocurrency market. Regulatory announcements, such as bans or restrictions, can also lead to sudden price drops, affecting the entire crypto landscape.

To reduce the effects of unpredictable black swan events, it's essential to diversify. Spreading investments across multiple cryptocurrencies and other asset classes can cushion losses when unexpected events occur. Additionally, maintaining a long-term perspective is essential. While black swan events can cause temporary setbacks, the cryptocurrency market has historically shown resilience, often bouncing back stronger after periods of turmoil.

Black swan events, by their very nature, defy prediction. Still, a well-thought-out approach can help you navigate these challenges with confidence. By combining preparedness, diversification, and informed decision-making, you can build a robust strategy to weather the impact of even the most unforeseen market disruptions.

CHAPTER 8
BUILDING CONFIDENCE FOR FUTURE INVESTMENTS

As a beginner, embracing lifelong learning is crucial to confidently navigating this dynamic industry. Staying relevant requires an open mind and a willingness to adapt to technological advancements. This chapter will equip you with the tools and resources to continually expand your knowledge base, ensuring you remain informed and empowered in your investment journey.

8.1 THE IMPORTANCE OF LIFELONG LEARNING IN CRYPTOCURRENCY

In the rapidly changing landscape of cryptocurrency, lifelong learning is your most valuable asset. The industry thrives on innovation, with new technologies and strategies emerging breathtakingly. Committing to continuous learning ensures that you remain at the forefront of these developments, ready to seize opportunities. This adaptability is not just about staying current; it's about cultivating a mindset that embraces change and seeks to understand it. In doing so, you position yourself not only as a participant but as an informed and strategic investor, capable of making decisions that align with your financial goals.

A wealth of educational platforms and resources is available to support your ongoing learning. Online courses, such as those offered by Coursera, provide structured and comprehensive insights into digital currencies, blockchain technology, and investment strategies. These courses, often taught by experts from top universities, offer a range of topics suitable for all levels, from beginners to more advanced learners. Additionally, podcasts and YouTube channels focused on cryptocurrency are excellent ways to stay informed about industry trends and hear from thought leaders. Shows like "The Pomp Podcast" and "Unchained" feature interviews with experts and provide in-depth analysis of the latest developments, ensuring you have access to diverse perspectives and insights.

Reading industry publications is another effective way to deepen your understanding of the cryptocurrency market. Subscribing to newsletters from reputable sources keeps you updated with the latest news, helping you identify emerging trends and make informed investment decisions. Following industry reports can also provide valuable insights into broader market movements and forecasts. These publications often include expert commentary and analysis, offering a comprehensive overview of the factors influencing the market. Regularly engaging with such content enhances your ability to anticipate changes and respond strategically.

Resources for Ongoing Education

- **Online Courses:** Explore Coursera's offerings for comprehensive learning in cryptocurrency and blockchain.
- **Podcasts:** Tune into "The Pomp Podcast" and "Unchained" for expert insights and discussions.
- **Newsletters:** Subscribe to industry-leading newsletters for the latest news and trends.
- **Forums:** Join BitcoinTalk for community discussions and networking.

Engaging with these resources empowers you to continue learning and adapting, ensuring you remain confident and informed in your cryptocurrency investments.

8.2 OPPORTUNITIES FOR CAREER ADVANCEMENT IN CRYPTOCURRENCY

The cryptocurrency industry rapidly evolves, creating a robust job market with opportunities. As digital currencies gain traction, the demand for specialized skills grows, opening doors to numerous career paths. Blockchain developers are at the forefront, crafting the frameworks upon which cryptocurrencies operate. Their role involves designing, implementing, and supporting blockchain applications, requiring proficiency in programming languages such as Solidity, Python, and JavaScript. These languages are the foundation of blockchain technology, empowering developers to build smart contracts and decentralized applications. The need for crypto analysts and consultants is also on the rise as businesses seek expertise to navigate the complexities of digital assets. These professionals analyze market trends, assess risks, and provide strategic advice, helping organizations make informed investment decisions in the volatile crypto landscape.

Gaining the right skills and certifications can significantly enhance your career prospects in the crypto industry. Understanding blockchain architecture and mastering programming languages like Solidity is crucial for those interested in technical roles. Certifications in blockchain technology, such as those offered by industry leaders, can validate your expertise and make you stand out in a competitive job market. These credentials demonstrate a commitment to the field and provide a structured pathway to acquiring the knowledge necessary for success. As the industry matures, practical experience and continuous learning become increasingly valuable, underscoring the importance of staying current with technological advancements and best practices.

The pathways within the crypto sector are diverse, extending beyond traditional tech roles. Fintech startups offer vibrant environments where innovation thrives and creativity is encouraged. These companies often look for individuals with a passion for technology and a willingness to experiment with new ideas. Additionally, roles in regulatory and compliance sectors are gaining importance as governments and organizations strive to establish clear guidelines for digital currencies. Professionals in these roles ensure businesses adhere to legal standards, balancing innovation with regulatory requirements. The intersection of finance and technology creates many opportunities for those interested in shaping the future of money.

Leveraging your existing skills can be a powerful way to transition into a crypto career. Marketing professionals, for instance, can apply their expertise to blockchain companies, developing strategies highlighting digital currencies' unique value propositions. Grasping the intricacies of the crypto market enables marketers to create captivating narratives that connect with audiences and boost engagement. Similarly, accountants specializing in crypto tax can offer valuable services to individuals and businesses navigating the intricate tax implications of digital assets. Their ability to interpret complex regulations and provide clear guidance is essential in an industry where compliance is critical. By building on your skills and gaining targeted knowledge, you can carve out a niche in the burgeoning crypto sector.

Career Advancement Checklist

- Blockchain Development: Enhance skills in Solidity and Python for development roles.
- Certifications: Seek blockchain certifications to validate expertise.
- Fintech Opportunities: Explore roles in innovative startups and compliance sectors.
- Skill Transition: Apply marketing or accounting skills to crypto-focused companies.

Consider these opportunities as gateways to a career in an industry reshaping the financial landscape. As you navigate these paths, remember that your skills can be adapted to fulfill the needs of this dynamic and fast-growing field.

8.3 BALANCING CRYPTOCURRENCY WITH OTHER FINANCIAL PRIORITIES

Picture your financial portfolio as a carefully nurtured garden, where each section symbolizes a distinct investment type, all collaborating to form a balanced and flourishing ecosystem. In investing, diversification is akin to planting a variety of crops; it ensures that the success of your financial garden does not rely on the unpredictable nature of a single asset class. While cryptocurrencies present exciting opportunities, balancing them with traditional assets like stocks and bonds can provide added stability and risk mitigation. These instruments have long been the mainstay of investment portfolios, providing stability and steady growth. Real estate is another possible component, offering tangible value and income generation through rental properties. By integrating more assets, you create a financial landscape that is both resilient and adaptable to changing market conditions.

Incorporating cryptocurrency into your overall financial plan requires thoughtful consideration and strategic allocation. Start by determining what percentage of your portfolio you wish to allocate to digital currencies. This allocation should align with your risk tolerance and investment objectives while accounting for the inherent volatility of the crypto market. A common strategy is to allocate a smaller portion, such as 5-10%, allowing you to tap into potential growth without overexposing yourself to excessive risk. Regularly reviewing and adjusting your investments is equally essential. Market conditions change, and your portfolio should evolve accordingly. Periodically reviewing your asset allocation ensures that your investments align with your financial goals and risk tolerance. This proactive strategy helps protect your assets while optimizing their growth potential.

The use of a financial advisor can be of benefit when navigating the complexities of a diversified portfolio. These professionals offer personalized guidance, drawing on their expertise to help you make informed decisions. Consulting an advisor can provide valuable insights into asset allocation, ensuring your investments are appropriately diversified. They also offer expertise in understanding your investments' tax implications and legal considerations, particularly about cryptocurrencies, which can be complex and ever-changing. Working with a financial advisor enables you to make informed, strategic decisions that align with your long-term goals, offering peace of mind and confidence in your investment strategy.

Setting clear financial priorities is critical in aligning your investments with your life goals. Consider what you hope to achieve financially, whether saving for retirement, funding education, or making significant purchases like a home. These goals provide direction, guide your investment decisions, and help you allocate resources effectively. For instance, if retirement savings are a priority, you might focus on building a diversified portfolio that balances growth with stability. If education funding is your goal, you might explore investments with a shorter time horizon, ensuring funds are available when needed. By clearly defining your financial priorities, you create a roadmap that steers your investments toward achieving meaningful outcomes.

Financing cryptocurrency with other financial priorities is ultimately about creating a harmonious portfolio that reflects your values and aspirations. It's about recognizing the potential of digital currencies while appreciating the stability offered by traditional assets. It's about making informed decisions, supported by expert guidance, that align with your life goals. Embrace the diversity of investment options available to you, and cultivate a portfolio that withstands the test of time and propels you toward financial success.

8.4 DEVELOPING CRITICAL THINKING SKILLS FOR BETTER DECISION-MAKING

Imagine embarking on a journey where each decision has the power to shape your financial future. In investing, critical thinking acts as your compass, helping you navigate the complexities of the market. It empowers you to assess information objectively, ensuring your choices are based on reason rather than emotion or bias. By sharpening this skill, you can avoid cognitive biases—those subtle, often unconscious influences that distort your judgment. Critical thinking enables you to analyze data, challenge assumptions, and make informed, logical decisions that align with your investment goals. It's about achieving clarity and focus, cutting through the noise to uncover the essential truths that drive successful investing.

To enhance your critical thinking skills, consider adopting techniques that cultivate a more analytical mindset. Scenario analysis is one such method. You can better anticipate potential challenges and opportunities by envisioning various outcomes and their impacts. This practice encourages flexibility, allowing you to adjust your strategies as new information emerges. Reflective thinking is equally valuable, prompting you to examine your decisions and their reasoning. This introspection fosters self-awareness, helping you identify patterns in your thought processes and refine them over time. Engaging in these practices sharpens your analytical skills and builds resilience, preparing you to confidently navigate the cryptocurrency market's unpredictable nature.

Questioning assumptions is a cornerstone of critical thinking. In the fast-paced world of cryptocurrency, where speculation runs high, it's vital to challenge the beliefs that underpin market predictions and investment advice. Analyze the basis of these assumptions: Do credible data support them, or are they driven by hype and speculation? Similarly, assess the validity of expert opinions, recognizing that even seasoned professionals can be mistaken. By scrutinizing the foundations of these insights, you cultivate a more nuanced understanding of the market. This skepticism is not about dismissing expert knowledge but seeking a deeper, more comprehensive view considering multiple perspectives. It empowers you to make decisions grounded in reality, not conjecture.

Evidence-based decision-making is the hallmark of effective investing. In a landscape brimming with information, discernment is key. Data-driven analysis provides a solid foundation for your strategies, ensuring they are informed by rigorous research and statistics. Compare historical data and trends to uncover patterns that might inform future movements. This approach enhances your understanding of market dynamics and instills confidence in your decisions. By grounding your choices in evidence, you mitigate the risks of impulsive actions driven by emotion or misinformation. This disciplined approach fosters a more strategic mindset, enabling you to navigate the complexities of investing with assurance and clarity.

In developing these skills, remember that critical thinking is a continuous process. It evolves with experience and reflection, becoming more refined as you encounter new challenges and insights. Embrace this journey of growth, knowing that each decision, whether successful or not, contributes to your development as a thoughtful, informed investor. As you cultivate critical thinking, you lay the groundwork for a more deliberate and practical approach to managing your investments, preparing you to thrive in cryptocurrency's dynamic and ever-changing world.

8.5 INSPIRING STORIES: SUCCESS AND LESSONS FROM INVESTORS

The cryptocurrency world is filled with stories of remarkable success, which can be a beacon of inspiration for those just starting. Take the early Bitcoin adopters, for example. These individuals, intrigued by the prospect of a decentralized currency, invested when Bitcoin was merely a novel experiment. They saw potential where others saw risk, and their patience paid off handsomely. Many were visionaries, not deterred by the volatility that often accompanies innovation. Their foresight and willingness to embrace uncertainty paved the way for substantial returns, turning modest investments into significant wealth. They weren't just lucky; they were strategic, often holding onto their assets through tumultuous market cycles, trusting in the technology and its potential to revolutionize finance.

In the realm of altcoins, stories of success are equally compelling. Investors who ventured beyond Bitcoin and explored emerging cryptocurrencies have found themselves in lucrative positions. Consider those who invested in Ethereum during its early days. Recognizing its potential to support decentralized applications, these investors understood that Ethereum was more than another digital coin. As the platform grew, so did their investments. Their success was not just about picking the right coin but understanding the underlying technology and its real-world applications. They exemplified the importance of research and the ability to see beyond immediate gains, focusing on the long-term potential of the projects they supported. This approach requires a deep understanding of the market and a belief in the transformative power of the technology.

Successful investors often share common traits that contribute to their achievements. Patience stands out as a fundamental quality. In a market characterized by rapid fluctuations, the ability to hold steady and resist the urge to react impulsively is invaluable. Perseverance is equally essential. Many successful investors have experienced setbacks yet remain committed to their vision. They understand that growth often comes from adversity and that challenges are disguised opportunities. Continuous learning and adaptability are also key. The crypto market evolves rapidly, and those who thrive stay informed and are willing to adjust their strategies as the landscape shifts. They are not rigid in thinking but embrace change and innovation, viewing it as a pathway to new possibilities.

Learning from challenges and failures is a crucial part of any investment journey. Market downturns, for instance, can be daunting, but they often provide the best lessons. When the market dips, successful investors don't panic. Instead, they analyze what went wrong, adapt their strategies, and prepare for the next opportunity. They understand that every downturn is temporary and recovery is often just around the corner. Consider the investor who took the time to reassess and refine their approach after suffering losses during a market crash. By reflecting on past mistakes, they gained valuable insights that shaped their future decisions, ultimately leading to greater success. This resilience and openness to learning from failure is what distinguishes successful investors. Drawing inspiration from these stories can be a powerful source of motivation.

CONCLUSION

Let's reflect on our path as we end our journey together. We've explored the fascinating world of cryptocurrency, from its basic definition to the technological marvel of blockchain. We've delved into the practical aspects of buying, selling, and safeguarding your digital assets. The book has guided you through crafting innovative investment strategies and understanding the potential and pitfalls of this evolving financial frontier. We've also touched on the future possibilities that blockchain technology holds beyond Bitcoin and cryptocurrencies.

Throughout this book, the key message has been clear: cryptocurrency is accessible to everyone, regardless of financial background. You don't need a fortune to start investing. The crucial element is making informed choices. You can achieve financial growth by adopting disciplined strategies and understanding the market. Remember, small, consistent steps often lead to the most significant gains.

It's natural to feel cautious about entering the world of cryptocurrency. Risks are part of any investment landscape. But with the tools and knowledge you've gained, you're well-prepared to face these challenges. Whether it's navigating volatility or understanding security measures, you now have a solid foundation to make confident decisions.

Now, it's time for action. With your newfound understanding, take the first step on your cryptocurrency journey. Start small, invest wisely, and continue learning. Engage with the crypto community. Share experiences, seek advice, and remain curious. The world of digital finance is dynamic and ever-changing. Staying informed and adaptable will keep you ahead of the curve.

Looking to the future, the possibilities within the cryptocurrency and blockchain realm are limitless. From decentralized finance to smart contracts, the innovations on the horizon are set to transform industries and redefine financial systems. By staying open-minded and proactive, you will be ready to seize these opportunities.

I am writing to express my gratitude for joining me on this journey. Your dedication to learning is commendable, and I hope this book has been both enlightening and empowering. Your feedback is invaluable, and I invite you to share your thoughts and experiences, as it will help shape future content.

As you move forward, remember that the knowledge you've acquired is a powerful tool. Use it to take charge of your financial future. Embrace the opportunities that come your way and let informed decisions and strategic thinking guide your journey. The digital finance landscape is yours to explore, and the potential for success is within your grasp.

Thank you for allowing me to be a part of your journey. I look forward to hearing about your experiences and successes in cryptocurrency. Let this begin a lifelong adventure in financial exploration and growth.

REFERENCES

Nakamoto, S. (2008). *Bitcoin: A peer-to-peer electronic cash system.* https://bitcoin.org/bitcoin.pdf

Ethereum Foundation. (2024, April 22). *Introduction to smart contracts.* Ethereum. https://ethereum.org/en/developers/docs/smart-contracts/

Franck, T. (2024, May 29). *Bitcoin, altcoins, meme coin differences explained.* CNBC. https://www.cnbc.com/2024/05/29/bitcoin-altcoins-meme-coin-differences-explained.html

Investopedia. (2024, September 16.). *Blockchain facts: What is it, how it works, and how it can benefit your business?* Investopedia. https://www.investopedia.com/terms/b/blockchain.asp

Investopedia. (2024, December). *Best crypto exchanges and apps for December 2024.* Investopedia. https://www.investopedia.com/best-crypto-exchanges-5071855

Material Bitcoin. (n.d.). *How to set up a hardware wallet: Step by step.* Material Bitcoin. https://materialbitcoin.com/en/blog/set-up-hardware-wallet/?srsltid=AfmBOooXwniXNQ06RR-vtI7-TKAIPiVzbdf6UDTCPgL06s-AfkH5bSIA0

Atlantic Council. (n.d.). *Cryptocurrency regulation tracker.* Atlantic Council. https://www.atlanticcouncil.org/programs/geoeconomics-center/cryptoregulationtracker/

Federal Trade Commission. (n.d.). *What to know about cryptocurrency and scams.* Federal Trade Commission. https://consumer.ftc.gov/articles/what-know-about-cryptocurrency-and-scams#

Bankrate. (2024, November 20). *How to start investing in cryptocurrency: A guide for beginners.* Bankrate. https://www.bankrate.com/investing/how-to-invest-in-cryptocurrency-beginners-guide/

Business Insider. (2024, December). *Best cryptocurrency exchanges of 2024.* Business Insider. https://www.businessinsider.com/personal-finance/investing/best-crypto-bitcoin-exchanges

Swiss Money. (2024). *Crypto transaction fees: A beginner's guide.* Swiss Money. https://swissmoney.com/cryptocurrency-transaction-fees

Internal Revenue Service. (n.d.). *Digital assets.* IRS. https://www.irs.gov/businesses/small-businesses-self-employed/digital-assets

REFERENCES

Honeybricks. (n.d.). *Ultimate guide to diversifying your crypto portfolio.* Honeybricks. https://www.honeybricks.com/learn/crypto-portfolio-diversification

Financial Crime Academy. (n.d.). *A comprehensive guide to effective risk management.* Financial Crime Academy. https://financialcrimeacademy.org/cryptocurrency-risk-management/

Kriptomat. (n.d.). *Trading psychology: How to manage emotions and decisions.* Kriptomat. https://kriptomat.io/finance-investing/trading-psychology-how-to-manage-emotions-and-decisions/

Bitcoin.com. (2024). *Discover the best analytical tools for cryptocurrency in 2024.* Bitcoin.com. https://www.bitcoin.com/analytical-tools/

CoinDCX. (n.d.). *How to set 'SMART' crypto investment goals.* CoinDCX. https://coindcx.com/blog/cryptocurrency/crypto-investing-strategy/

Crypto.com. (n.d.). *Four phases of the crypto market cycle.* Crypto.com. https://crypto.com/en/university/four-phases-crypto-market-cycle

Iconomi. (2024). *Short-term vs. long-term crypto investment strategies.* Iconomi. https://www.iconomi.com/blog/short-term-vs-long-term-crypto-investing

Token Metrics. (n.d.). *10 best crypto tools for investors and traders.* Token Metrics. https://www.tokenmetrics.com/blog/crypto-tools

Deloitte. (n.d.). *Using blockchain to drive supply chain transparency.* Deloitte. https://www2.deloitte.com/us/en/pages/operations/articles/blockchain-supply-chain-innovation.html

Zhang, Q., & Soni, S. (2020). *Blockchain smart contracts: Applications, challenges, and opportunities.* National Institutes of Health. https://pmc.ncbi.nlm.nih.gov/articles/PMC8053233/

Investopedia. (n.d.). *What is decentralized finance (DeFi) and how does it work?.* Investopedia. https://www.investopedia.com/decentralized-finance-defi-5113835

Popper, N. (2021, April 13). *NFTs are shaking up the art world. They may be warming up the planet too.* The New York Times. https://www.nytimes.com/2021/04/13/climate/nft-climate-change.html

ECCU. (n.d.). *A cybersecurity guide to safely storing your cryptocurrency.* ECCU. https://www.eccu.edu/blog/cybersecurity/cryptocurrency-cybersecurity-how-to-store-your-crypto-safely/

Li, H., & Liu, Y. (2023). *The environmental footprint of Bitcoin mining across the globe.* Geophysical Research Letters, 50(10), e2023EF003871. https://agupubs.onlinelibrary.wiley.com/doi/full/10.1029/2023EF003871

REFERENCES

Investopedia. (2024, July 28). *How to deal with crypto FOMO*. Investopedia. https://www.investopedia.com/deal-with-crypto-fomo-6455103

CoinDCX. (2024, November 12). *Understanding crypto volatility: Why it's so high and how to manage it*. CoinDCX. https://coindcx.com/blog/cryptocurrency/understanding-crypto-volatility-and-how-to-manage-it/

Coursera. (n.d.). *Best cryptocurrency courses & certificates [2025]*. Coursera. https://www.coursera.org/courses?query=cryptocurrency

NinjaPromo. (2024, December 24). *Top 13 crypto podcasts: Best Bitcoin & blockchain insights*. NinjaPromo. https://ninjapromo.io/the-best-crypto-podcasts

CCN. (2024, November 29). *Crypto jobs are booming again: Top skills you need for 2025*. CCN. https://www.ccn.com/education/crypto/crypto-jobs-skills-2025/

The Motley Fool. (2024, March 24). *How to create a well-balanced crypto portfolio*. The Motley Fool. https://www.fool.com/investing/stock-market/market-sectors/financials/cryptocurrency-stocks/crypto-portfolio/

Printed in Great Britain
by Amazon